Pr...
Catch ...
God's Supernatural

"If you only catch God's power, *you* will do the same works as Jesus! As you read *Catch and Release God's Supernatural*, the same presence of God on Jesus will come upon you!"

SID ROTH
HOST, *IT'S SUPERNATURAL!*

"These Kingdom power secrets are secrets God wants *everyone* to know! Brother Andrew explains them in such an understandable way as he teaches us how anyone can use them. This book is *so* vital for to-day's believers. With all that is happening in the world today, you need this book. I highly recommend *Catch and Release God's Supernatural* to all who desire the manifested power of God in their daily life!"

TOD TRUITT
SENIOR PASTOR, LIFE CHURCH

"The apostolic call and mission of the first-century church and our mission and call today are to understand, teach, and release the mysteries of God. These mysteries include, but are not limited to, the revelation that we are no longer to see ourselves as Jew or Greek, slave or free, male or female in Christ, but we are *one new man* in the earth. Another deeply important revelation that must be released is the availability to manifest God's supernatural in and through our lives . . . not through superstar ministers, but via all members of the body of Christ. Dr. Nkoyoyo's latest work, *Catch and Release God's Supernatural*, will lead you into new dimensions of the mysteries of God and the release of His supernatural in your life."

DR. STAN DEKOVEN
FOUNDER AND PRESIDENT, VISION INTERNATIONAL UNIVERSITY

"The Apostle Paul mentioned in 1 Corinthians 2:4 that his message was not preached with persuasive words of wisdom, but the demonstration of the Holy Spirit's power. As saints in the kingdom of God, many understand that wisdom and knowledge is power, but Dr. Andrew wants to show us that demonstration of the kingdom is not merely power, it is powerful. In Dr. Andrew Nkoyoyo's new book, *Catch and Release God's Supernatural: Keys to Operating in God's Miracles, Healing, and Power*, readers are given keys to open up the divine mysteries of God, to experience the power of the Holy Spirit in their lives and in the lives of others. Andrew shows the believer how to move from knowing what a believer can do to actually doing it, all to the glory of God. Having worked closely alongside Dr. Andrew, my wife and I have seen and experienced his ministry, and it's with honor that we proudly recommend this book."

PASTORS JIMMIE AND LUCRETIA CHURCH
BYFORCE MINISTRIES

"Dr. Andrew once again has made it possible that every leader and believer who reads this book will never be the same again in their lives. *Catch and Release God's Supernatural* is practical, and this kingdom book awakens every part of us to enter into a supernatural experience with God. A must-read in the body of Christ right now."

DR. MIKE KINGSLEY
FOUNDER AND PRESIDENT OF WORLD TRUMPET TV NETWORK

What a timely book! In *Catch and Release God's Supernatural*, Andrew mentors you on how to catch hold of God and operate in ways you never thought possible. Your faith can't help but increase as your armor acquires several more layers. This isn't a book you want to ignore but one that should become the go-to manual for every believer who wants to be used by God for healing and miracles!

SHERRIE CLARK
AWARD-WINNING, BEST-SELLING AUTHOR, EDITOR
CEO, STOREHOUSE MEDIA GROUP LLC

CATCH & RELEASE
—— GOD'S ——
SUPERNATURAL

Keys to Operating in
GOD'S MIRACLES,
HEALING, and POWER

DR. ANDREW M. NKOYOYO

Published by:
Spirit Life Publishing, LLC
Myspiritlifepublishing.com

ISBN: 978-1-7358190-0-6 (paperback)
ISBN: 978-1-7358190-1-3 (eBook)
LCCN: 2020923275

Printed in the United States of America.

1 3 5 7 9 10 8 6 4 2

I dedicate this book to my wife Mona, the love of my life, the woman of my dreams, and my best friend.

I also dedicate this book to my awesome children Jasper, Petra, Sardius, and Jade.

CONTENTS

Acknowledgments

THIS BOOK is not my work as a solo writer. Many people have helped me to become the person I am today so that I'm able to share this book with you. In a practical sense, they are my collaborators on this project:

My wife **Mona**—You're a glorious gift to me. When God gave you to me, He gave me His best, and I am richer for it. You know me more than anyone, love me unconditionally, and have helped me become the person I am today. Your persevering support and sacrifice are my inspiration, and I dedicate my life to you.

My children **Jasper, Petra, Sardius, and Jade**—You are God's precious gift to me and my treasure. Daily, you teach me what unconditional love is. Being your father is my greatest honor and reward. I love and cherish each of you dearly.

The late Dr. Morris Cerullo—Thank you for training me and imparting to me a double portion of the anointing of an apostle and prophet that is on your life and calling to fulfill the ministry of a New Testament apostle and prophet of Jesus. My life and ministry have never been the same since that day in August 1997.

Bishop Charles Nsubuga—Thank you for being a godly spiritual father and friend and for always being there for me.

Pastor Robert Kayanja, Pastor Emelda Namutebi, Pastor Isaac Kiwewesi—Thank you for being great role models for me in living a life of faith, walking in the power of God, and imparting the anointing upon me.

Darlene Dimitrovski—Thank you for helping me compile and edit my preaching and teaching transcriptions, which made it much easier for me to eliminate and add content to this book.

Pastor Tod and Lori Truit—Your consistent encouragement and prayer helped to make this book possible.

Allen and Patty Schroeder, Pastor Jimmie Church, Tracy Keeton, Darlene Dimitrovski, my amazing team and friends at Kingdom Impact Ministry. Thank you for coming alongside me with your tireless support, prayers, and service for people and God's Kingdom.

Stephen and Mary Lindow, Garth and Kirstein Schulthies, Todd & Bonnie Barbey, Barry and Ronah Francolino, Bill & Pat O'Dell, Emagene Calvart, Tim Tyler—Thank you for your steadfast love and persevering support to us.

Sherrie Clark—Thank you and your team at Storehouse Media Group for your diligent work of editing and publishing this book.

FOREWORD
By Dr. Ché Ahn

WE ARE LIVING in an extraordinary era in history. All around the world, God is looking for believers who are ready to receive a fresh outpouring of His glory (Habakkuk 2:14). Many Christians today are hungry for the things of God and desire to experience the greater works of Jesus. Yet not all are prepared to act as vessels for the power and glory of God.

In his new book, *Catch and Release God's Supernatural*, Andrew Nkoyoyo offers an open invitation for you to partner with the mighty work of the Holy Spirit in your generation. As a member of Harvest International Ministry (our global apostolic network advancing the Kingdom of God in over seventy nations), Andrew truly has a heart to preach the gospel of the kingdom with signs and wonders following and help to fulfill the Great Commission by making disciples of nations (Matthew 28:18–20).

This book reflects the call of God on the author's life as it is full of testimonies demonstrating God's goodness and divine power. Each chapter weaves together personal stories with scriptural truths that will encourage and equip believers to walk in the same anointing that was at work in Jesus's ministry on Earth. If you want to be activated in the supernatural, take hold of these biblically based keys to releasing God's power into your life and put the Word of God into practice.

God wants every believer to walk in a greater measure of miracles as we flow in His love and are empowered by the Holy Spirit. *Catch and Release God's Supernatural* carries the DNA of revival, and I believe it will help you act on your faith and see the Kingdom of God come into your sphere of influence like never before.

Dr. Ché Ahn
Founder and President, Harvest International Ministry
Founding and Senior Pastor, Harvest Rock Church, Pasadena, California
International Chancellor, Wagner University
Founder, Ché Ahn Ministries

Introduction

ARE YOU TIRED of depending on other people's faith, anointing, and relationship with God to experience healing, miracles, power, and breakthroughs in your life?

If you feel afraid to set out because you think you will fail or not see any results, if you feel frustrated because you have prayed, believed, and done everything you know how to do but your prayers and actions seem to have gone unanswered by God, if you feel unworthy or that you don't measure up to being able to access God's supernatural in your own life or for others by your faith, anointing, or prayers, then you're not alone.

I have come across many dear Christians in my travels who have repeatedly asked, "Brother Andrew, can you show me how to catch and release the supernatural works of God in my own life and for other people? Can you teach me how I can become fully equipped to be used by God to walk in the authority Jesus delegated to me and to hear God's voice for myself, to be able to unleash His power with miracles, signs, and wonders following me as promised in the Scriptures?"

If you're ready to go from frustration, fear, confusion, doubt, unbelief, and compromise, if you're ready to go where you need to be experiencing the supernatural miracles of God in any area of your life by your faith, action, and prayers, then I have a solution for you.

There is just one thing that is standing between you and the life you desire, one of miracles, healing, victory, breakthrough, success, blessings, and reaching the next level of your full potential in life or whatever God has called you to do—and that is the power of God or the anointing you have. Without them, these yearnings cannot occur.

Thirty-four years ago, I was a new believer with a call from God to preach the gospel, to heal the sick, cast out devils, and set the captives free. But there was one problem. No matter how much I preached and prayed for people, no one got healed or set free. I started to get frustrated and discouraged and doubted the call of God.

I wondered, *What am I doing wrong? Maybe I don't have enough faith. Maybe I don't have the right spiritual gifts. Maybe I should give it up.*

In my desperate struggle to find a solution to my need to operate in the supernatural of God, I decided to find a mentor. I searched for those men and women of God who were walking in miracles, healing, power, signs, and wonders. I sat under their ministries and observed, hoping to learn something from them. And I did. I received a revelation of the one thing that all these servants of God had that I didn't have—the power or the anointing of the Holy Spirit upon their lives!

So, I set out to learn how to connect to the power of God and how to unlock it in my life. Also, I discovered that any Christian can walk in the supernatural through the power of God if they learn how to use the kingdom's power keys to unleash it in and through their lives.

I began to develop a lifestyle of power in my own life while practicing the keys, secrets, and methods I teach in this book, and that's when I had the breakthrough. At the age of fifteen, I stepped out in power by faith, and a blind beggar was healed instantly in the marketplace. Hundreds of people at the very least got saved that day, and my miracle ministry was born. When this happened, I wasn't trained by any school, nor was I licensed or ordained for ministry. I didn't even do any ministry in our church. I was just a teenager loving Jesus and people and sharing the gospel at school, on the streets, and in the marketplace.

WHY I WROTE THIS BOOK

My goal with this book is to help mobilize and equip the saint movement, which is comprised of everyday people like you and me, and to operate in the power of God that releases miracles, healing, victories, and blessings in their own lives and for others.

I wrote this book to take the mystery out of the power of God for any Christian who thought that it was only for ministry, given to a few chosen people serving in the Church. I'll show you how the power of God is successful both in your everyday Christian life and in your ministry. You'll see how it's available for you and any follower of Christ to enjoy.

WHAT YOU'LL LEARN

Consider this book your key ring and me your mentor. I'll show you each of the keys and how you too can use them to access a lifestyle of the supernatural and power of God upon your life regardless of your calling or maturity level.

I'll teach you how to use the same keys, secrets, methods, and steps that allowed me to go from a struggling, mediocre Christian to changing my own life and hundreds of thousands of people around the world with the supernatural-working power through my miracle crusades, conferences, and church services for the past thirty-three years. Now, I'm going to mentor you by:

- Taking you on a journey using testimonies and stories of my personal experiences to show you the kingdom power keys in action and how to apply them with step-by-step guidance.

- Revealing what the power of God is, why you need it, and the results of that power in and through your life.
- Telling you how to connect into God's power and how to develop a lifestyle where you're full of power every day.
- Then explaining step by step how to experience and release God's supernatural and power in and through your own life to impact other people.

I've experienced several miracle healings in my own body as I've followed and applied what I teach you in this book. You'll learn how I was miraculously healed from an underactive thyroid (hypothyroidism), type 2 diabetes, received a creative miracle of a new liver that was in failure, and healed of many injuries from a car accident. You'll read how I received the manifestations as well as the details of other powerful stories. If what I teach worked for me, it will work for you too.

I promise that if you put into practice the knowledge you receive in this book, you'll have many opportunities to experience God's supernatural in your life, be victorious, and walk in God's power to heal the sick and set the captives free.

Are you ready for the next level of miracles, healing, and power in your life? If so, then let's get started so that you can see how to catch and release God's supernatural right now!

The kingdom power secrets, keys, methods, and steps you're about to read have proven results. Each chapter provides new secrets that will enlighten you to take action to unlock power from heaven that's already in you.

The content in this book is part my comprehensive six-week online training course called the School of the Anointing. Go beyond this book and get the course today. Check it out here:

https://www.kingdomimpactministry.org/yes

SECTION I

THE POWER

CHAPTER 1

Walking in God's Power Is Attainable

ONE JANUARY AFTERNOON in 1986, I heard a gentle voice speak to my heart as one would talk to a friend. I found out later from my mother that it was the voice of the Holy Spirit.

He asked me three questions. The first was "Have you thought about your eternity?" Though my mother had taught me about "eternity," I didn't fully understand what it meant.

Then I heard the second question. "Have you made plans for your future?"

I didn't answer it, but in my mind, I thought I wanted to be a doctor, make a lot of money, marry a pretty girl, and have eleven children (my own soccer team—not literally).

It wasn't until He asked me the third question that I realized my understanding of the future was so superficial. "Okay, Andrew. When you've achieved all your dreams and desires in this life, and when your life here on Earth is no more, where will you be?"

This last question got my attention; I didn't have an answer to it. All of sudden, everything my mother had taught me about eternity, spiritual death, forgiveness, repentance, and salvation all made sense. Immediately, my spiritual eyes were opened, and I realized my need for Jesus. I was gripped with conviction by the Spirit. So right there in my bedroom, I confessed my sins to God and invited Jesus into my heart as my Lord and Savior and have never looked back.

I wanted to change people's lives for Jesus, walk in the power of God, release miracles, signs, and wonders for myself and others, and do the very things that Jesus promised we would do as believers.

A few days after Jesus came into my life through a separate divine encounter, He called me into ministry saying, "Go to the nations and preach the gospel. Make disciples and raise for Me an army of end-time harvesters who are full of power. Equip the saints for ministry."

Remember, this was only days after I got saved. So I didn't even know what all that meant, but I said yes to God.

CHOOSE WHO YOU'LL SERVE

My parents never lived together and were never married to each other but did a great job raising me. I spent half of my school holidays with my father and the other half with my mother.

My family on my father's side were active and devout Catholics. He was a choir director, so we attended weekly masses. My siblings and I went through weeks of training to receive confirmation so that we could take communion and then serve at the altar.

When I was seven years old, my mother became a born-again believer and started teaching me the Word of God, how to pray, and took me to a Pentecostal/Charismatic church with her. Three years later, she began to preach in public meetings and consequently started a church and pastored it until five years ago when she retired from public ministry.

As a preacher's kid (PK), I was in church every Wednesday evening for Bible study and Sunday morning for worship services during school holidays. I knew about God but didn't have a relationship with Jesus until my encounter with the Holy Spirit that I shared with you at the beginning of this chapter. That sacred experience came shortly after my confirmation in the Catholic Church.

My mother was happy with my decision to become a born-again believer but not the rest of family, and neither were my friends.

My father asked, "What does born again mean anyway?"

After an hour or so of grueling questions and me explaining why and how I gave my life to Christ, he expressed his disappointment, disapproval, and contempt to what he called my new religion.

My stepmother intervened and reasoned with my father, saying, "At least he's not on drugs or has killed someone or committed a heinous crime. The boy just wants to love Jesus. Let him follow his Jesus."

But it all fell on deaf ears. My father thought for a few minutes. Then he turned to me. "You have another decision to make," he said. "You can denounce your new religion, stay Catholic, and be my son, or you can be born again but no longer be my son and part of this family. Your choice."

Back in 1986, to be born again was not very popular. We were considered those poor lunatics who preached on street corners and were given many unflattering labels and names.

I can only imagine what went through my father's mind when he gave me that ultimatum. Here he was a respected businessman, choir director, and leader in the community, and his son attended the papyrus wooden church with a dirt floor in the valley. That was a big step down from the stained-glass, high-ceiling church building with a tall steeple.

Can you imagine? I'm fourteen years old and faced with this life-changing decision. How do I decide? How do I choose? Family or God? How do I know if choosing God is the right decision?

I didn't know that answer, but what I did know was that deep down inside, I loved my relationship with the Lord more than I wanted to follow my family's religion. I wondered, *Is there a way to keep my relationship with the Lord and keep my family?*

In Africa, you're not only part of the family but also part of a tribe. Within that tribe is a clan. One's family name also tells others the group to which they belong. This so-called disgrace caused by my conversion affected not only my immediate family but also my tribe and the clan's people. As a result, I wasn't only disowned by my dad but also by the tribe and clan.

My biggest challenge was deciding whether my relationship with God was worth losing everything. I wondered what my life would look like a year, two years, five years, even ten years from now? I had no idea, but I had found true peace and joy in Jesus. For the first time in my young life, I had a purpose. I thought, *If Jesus did all that stuff in the Bible, He's able to help me.*

Again, it's not like I had days, weeks, or months to make my decision but a mere few hours. So, I chose Jesus and walked out of my father's house. I trusted God, but things got more difficult after that.

Thankfully, not everyone abandoned me, but life would never be the same. When I left my father's house, I went to church as usual and only shared my situation with Sam, a close friend who was a few years older than me. He would go with me whenever I went to share the gospel and pray for people.

After telling him my living predicament, he told me that his family had an unfinished basement I could live in, but there was a problem. They were not believers. He didn't know what they would say, but he invited me to go with him anyway after the church service and sleep in the basement. We'd figure out the details from there.

NOT HOMELESS (OR WAS I?)

Sam and I prayed for God's favor, and I went with him after church service that evening. When we arrived, everyone was already in bed. The next day, he introduced me to his auntie and shared with her my situation. He then asked her if I could stay in the basement, ensuring her of my good character, that I wouldn't be stealing from them, and I wouldn't be a burden to her family.

After presenting his case for me, she thought about it for a few minutes. Finally, she agreed.

They didn't have much to share in terms of food, but I sang praises for God's provision, thanking Him for this unfinished basement with concrete on the floor. It had nothing else—no bed, no pillow, no blanket, no mat.

It did have a broken window that increased the coldness in the room, but I praised God I wasn't homeless; I had a place to stay.

The only items I brought with me from my father's house were a bag of clothes, my school books, and my Bible. I slept on the concrete floor using the Bible as my pillow for a full year before God provided a small used mattress. The next-door neighbors were moving and didn't have room to take it with them, so they gave it to me.

WHERE IS THE GOD OF THE BIBLE?

Despite my circumstances, inside me was a fire, a burning desire to obey the call of God and to see people saved, healed, and delivered, and to make disciples of all nations. Before getting the mattress, I decided that instead of sleeping on this uncomfortable concrete floor, I would spend every night in the church praying. It became so much a part of my life that I continued spending every night in the church praying even after I got my mattress.

For those first three years, I found myself in a season of desperation for God. I couldn't explain it at the time, but now I know it was the burden of God driving me to seek Him until I met Him. I would spend every Monday through Sunday night in prayer. At around four o'clock in the morning, I would lie down on the pulpit for two hours of sleep and then go back to my basement, change my clothes, and go to school.

But again, because my father had disowned me, he wasn't paying my tuition for school anymore. My mother took care of me and did whatever she could, but she lived 400 miles away. For the rest, I had to just depend on God.

Here I was, fourteen years old, still in school, and disowned by my father, who lived over a mile away with a fully stocked refrigerator, warm bed, and anything else a boy of my age would need. Yet I lived in a basement that flooded whenever it rained heavily, and Uganda has rainy seasons between January through April and October through November when it sometimes rains all day every day. Because my mother lived on the opposite side of the country, I really had no family to call my own, except for a few people from church and my somewhat-adopted family.

Shortly after moving into that basement, I began sharing the gospel with whomever I met. I started with Sam's auntie. She didn't get saved right away. She had many questions, and by God's grace, I answered them, and the Holy Spirit went to work in her heart.

I also preached at school and then onto the streets or at the market before going to church. The next day, I'd do it all over again.

I lived in that basement for a total of two and a half years. Because of my relationship with Jesus, I had to endure this hardship. I remember days would go by without food. Sometimes Sam would boil me some hot water upstairs so that I could have dry black tea. Finding hot water to drink with tea was a big miracle, an absolute blessing.

MIRACLE OF BURNT BREAD

Then one cold morning in January during that time, Sam brought me a basket of burnt bread. It felt like Christmas! Drinking tea had been my nourishment before school, so I ate that bread that morning like it was my last meal. I hadn't had solid food in days.

After I ate, I asked Sam where the bread came from. He said, "There's a bakery at the very end of the street that gives away the bread that can't be sold, but you must be the first to get to the bakery. Be there around five o'clock in the morning."

This was huge. I had nourishment! I would walk to the bakery every Tuesday and arrive early enough before they threw out the bread that was burnt or couldn't be sold or before someone else took it. I was able to take it home and enjoy it. I went from starving for days, living on water or plain tea to eating burnt bread.

MY GREAT STRUGGLE TO BREAK THROUGH

In the same year I got saved, I started taking free correspondence Bible training through the Bible Way, a discipleship ministry out of England with an office in Kampala. It was fundamental, and I acquired a deeper understanding of the gospels.

But I still had this big challenge—how do I do the works of Jesus as He did in the gospels and as the apostles did in the Book of Acts? I went to church and saw Pastor Robert Kayanja, Pastor Emelda Namutebi, Bishop Charles Nsubuga, Pastor Isaac Kiwewesi, just to name a few, move effortlessly in miracles, signs, and wonders. They didn't even lay hands on the people most of the time.

Remember, I had the call from God to minister, and I was doing my best to share the gospel and pray for people. But no matter how much I preached and prayed for people in the marketplace, on the street, or at school, I didn't demonstrate the gospel in the Spirit and in the power like they did.

While preaching at my school and the local market in Kampala, people called me all kinds of names. They threw stones, tomatoes, and eggs at me. I was already timid, and as a result, I became embarrassed to share the gospel.

I started to think, *Maybe evangelizing in power is simply something that some people are born with. Maybe I just don't have enough faith. Maybe I'm not praying right. Maybe I don't have the right spiritual gifts. Maybe I should give it up.*

The enemy kept telling me all kinds of lies in my mind. So if you think you're stuck in a rut and are intimidated to set out to do God's plan, lay hands on the sick and believe God to heal them, cast out demons and set the captives free, or if you want to go from being a mere Christian to walking in God's supernatural power, miracles, and victory over the devil, and you feel you don't measure up, I know how you feel. I've been there too.

HOW I DISCOVERED THE ONE THING

Hoping to learn something, I started sitting under mighty men and women of God. I attended a miracle crusade conducted by T.L. and Daisy Osborn in Lugogo Stadium in Kampala, Uganda in the summer of 1986, and witnessed miracles, signs, and wonders happening so effortlessly through them. I watched videos, listened to cassette tapes, and read books written by other mighty men and women of God who were releasing His power, imagining myself also ministering in the same way to the masses.

Months later, I received a revelation from the Holy Spirit that would change my life and ministry forever: all of God's generals who operated in miracles, signs, and wonders, who demonstrated such spiritual authority and power over the devil, had something different than what I had. It really was one thing, just one thing they all had in common—the power of God or the anointing of the Spirit in and upon their lives that manifested through their ministries.

I realized that once you knew how to access God's power and how to operate in and with the anointing, you could release miracles, signs, and wonders daily like any spiritual general regardless of your calling or maturity level.

That is what I did. I started developing the lifestyle of the power of God by practicing the biblical keys, secrets, methods, and steps they followed in their lives and ministries. I then put into practice the tools I was learning in my own life and started ministering to others.

And I couldn't believe it worked!

MY FIRST INSTANT MIRACLE HEALING OF A BLIND BEGGAR

My previous efforts to help people through the gospel didn't produce any results, but this time I had a different mindset; I sought the power of God and yielded to the Holy Spirit. I asked Jesus to anoint me with His power to do His will, and He did.

My taking action on God's behalf activated the anointing with which the Holy Spirit was now clothing me. Now that I knew the truth about God's precious anointing, I became intentional to live the anointed life, to walk in and demonstrate the anointing.

Then I went back to the same marketplace where I had previously preached. I taught the same message entitled "Only Believe." (See Mark 5:35–37 and Luke 8:49–51.) I shared Christ and called people to get saved.

This time, though, it was different. A blind beggar came forward. I prayed for him, and for the first time, his eyes opened, and he could now see!

At the age of fifteen, I became a miracle witness for Christ with my first instant healing miracle of a blind beggar at the city center after I prayed for him. As a result of the move of God's power that day in 1987, my miracle ministry was born.

As I checked the blind beggar's eyes to confirm his miracle healing, the crowd grew from a few curious bystanders to the whole market fastened on me. I spoke through a horn speaker I had made out of cardboard. It wasn't enough for the thousands at the busy marketplace to hear me; they stated pressing forward to come closer to have a better look and to *listen* to what I was saying.

The crowd cheered when they witnessed the test results of the blind beggar's healing. I made a second call for salvation. Whereas before, people had thrown tomatoes and eggs at me, now hundreds of people got saved that day. Talk about power evangelism and soul winning! It felt like a dream, but it was real, and it was happening through me. I was not ordained, licensed, had no Bible college training or degree. I didn't have the right clothes or speak eloquently to move the crowd. The secret was the demonstration of the Spirit and power with tangible, verifiable miracles that made the way.

And on that day, all it took to go from struggling to victory and breakthrough was a single recognizable and visible miracle.

MY MIRACLE MINISTRY WAS BORN

At only fifteen years old, I began to walk in the power of God. The more I obeyed Him, the more His power increased upon my life and ministry.

In my book *Working the Works of God*, I share some of the miracle healing testimonies at my trade school and St. Francis Hospital Nsambya, among other places. I describe how God did miraculous signs and wonders, but the breakthrough came after I discovered the secret of God's power. That shifted everything for me.

A year later, I began to organize open-air evangelistic meetings at playgrounds and soccer fields. Everything I did focused around Hebrews 13:8: "Jesus is the same yesterday, today and forever." He is the same, and He's still doing the ministry of healing, miracles, and deliverance. He is the same Jesus today as He was yesterday.

Then one evening three years later, something amazing happened. At one of the gospel crusades, I noticed that people in the audience were getting healed and delivered from demonic oppression and evil spirts by the power of God without our ministry team or me praying for them.

At that point, I stopped laying hands on people one by one. I would pray a mass prayer over them, and God would touch them right where they were seated or standing. I still lay hands on people but only as the Lord leads me, especially in a big gathering.

DIVINE PROMOTION

Earlier in my story, I told you how I lived in the concrete basement for two and a half years. It was through the anointing that God promoted me from that basement to sleep in a real bed. Let me share with you how that came about.

One morning, a brother, Tom came to me and said, "The woman I work for as a housekeeper has suddenly taken ill. One of her legs has swollen up. Her condition looks like she has elephantiasis, but doctors don't know what to do to help her. She can't stand or walk on the swollen leg. I told her I'd ask you to go pray for her."

"Sure," I said, "let's go and pray for her right now."

It was about a thirty-minute walk to her house. As Tom, Sam, and I arrived, Tom went ahead of us to unlock the big metal outer door and then the inner doors to the living quarters. He then called for us to come in.

As I walked to the door where the sick woman was seated, something truly divine happened. She looked at me and said, "When you opened the door, suddenly, a big bright light filled the whole room, and I saw Jesus standing in front of me. My swollen leg went back to normal, and I was instantly healed."

The time it took for me to open the door and walk into her living room to where she sat happened in a matter of seconds. She had become utterly whole, standing on her two feet with her hands raised up to heaven, her body trembling under the power of Christ as she praised Him loudly.

"I'm healed! Praise God, I'm healed!" she rejoiced for several minutes. When she had collected herself together and sat back down, she repeated what had just happened. We glorified God together and gave Jesus the praise that was due Him for His love and power.

She then invited me to have tea with her and her sons and to pray for them too. Afterward, I said my goodbye and got up to leave. That's when she asked me if there was any thing she could do for me.

"No," I replied. "No, there isn't."

But Tom said, "Yes, there is. Andrew lives in an unfinished, flooding basement with only a mattress on the floor. He doesn't have a proper bed, no sheets, pillows, and blankets."

Then she asked me, "Would you come and live in the guest house on the other side of the compound? I would take care of all the expenses, including food, and Tom here will take care of you and make your stay as comfortable as possible. He'll cook for you, do your laundry, and everything you need done. You focus on serving God and whatever else you need to do."

That was a day of promotion from the unlivable basement condition to a fully furnished house with a helper. All it took was the demonstration of the power.

Now you might say, "Yes, the woman got miraculously healed, and you didn't even pray for her. How is the anointing connected with that?"

Acts 10:38 helps us to see this clearly: "How God anointed Jesus of Nazareth with the Holy Ghost and with power: who went about doing good, and healing all that were oppressed of the devil; for God was with him."

God was with Jesus through the anointing He had placed upon His life. In the same manner, Jesus is with you and me through the power He has put in us. God in His infinite mercy will sometimes open someone's eyes to Jesus who is with you. That's what happened to this dear woman—her eyes had been opened to Jesus with me. She saw that although He was the One who performed the healing, He used my vessel to carry His anointing.

This was the first time something like that happened through me, but it wouldn't be the last. Since then, many people have told me that they had seen Jesus in my crusades, conferences, services, and on the streets, even when I wasn't doing ministry. It has nothing to do with you and me. It's not because some people are holier than others. I wasn't all of a sudden better than anybody then nor am I now for that matter.

I shared my story to show you that it doesn't matter who you are, where you're from, what you desire to do in life, what your maturity level is, or what you're called to do. The power of God is the solution.

Fast forward to today. I have been privileged to be invited to minister alongside my heroes. What a blessing it is to minister around the world to 10,000 and 50,000 people at a time and witness multitudes immediately changed by the power of the Holy Spirit.

I can't tell you how fulfilling it is to be God's transforming vessel to take someone's life from bondage to freedom—instantly—without even thinking about it.

It's a dream come true to see people experience the miracles and blessings that Jesus purchased for them with His own life and freely gives to them through the anointing.

No matter what drives you to experience God's best, to walk in miracles, signs, and wonders, the power of God is the key.

THE RELATIONSHIP WITH MY FATHER RESTORED

Do you remember how my father had rejected and disowned me because of my faith in Jesus? Well, in the beginning of 1999, he began to come around.

I was finishing my mission to South Africa when I called him in Uganda to wish him a happy New Year. He seemed glad to hear from me. I told him that I would be in Uganda for two weeks before I traveled to the United Kingdom and that I would love to take him out to lunch. He agreed. That was a major step in our relationship.

We had not had that kind of fellowship in at least ten years. We met at a restaurant near his office. I got there early to make sure we got a table in a quiet part of the restaurant. A few minutes after I was seated, he arrived.

We shook hands and sat down. I didn't know where to start or what to talk about, so I asked him how he was doing and how my younger siblings were doing.

For a few minutes, he told me about his life and the health issues he was experiencing. He also told me about the family and how everyone was fairing.

Then suddenly, he leaned forward and said, "I have waited for this moment for a long time. I want to apologize for everything bad I said to you, for disowning and abandoning you. I thought you were ruining your life following Jesus like you did. I was wrong, and I can see what He has done in your life. I'm proud of you."

I told him I forgave him the same day he disowned me and have been praying for him since.

It was as if a ton of breaks had been lifted off his shoulders. You could see his countenance and tone of voice change. He had been secretly following what I was doing in ministry, looking for banners, posters, and ads and listening to radio announcements to see if I was involved in any upcoming events.

God healed our long-estranged relationship that afternoon. We enjoyed a delightful lunch and conversation for several hours.

For the next three years, we continued to talk as often as the time difference with my travels to different countries would allow.

MY FATHER GETS SAVED

Now that our relationship was restored, my father would call and ask me to pray for his business and to let him know if God showed me something. He was in the cargo shipping and forwarding business with offices at the Entebbe International Airport and other major points of entry into Uganda. He didn't call it prophetic advice, but that's what it was. I was happy to share insights from God about his business.

On one instance in 2002, he called seeking advice about whether to get involved with a multinational shipping company from Denmark. As we finished the conversation, he wondered how I could get insight about people and details I didn't know about.

I told him God loved him and that He was interested in him and every aspect of his life. I added that the insights I was receiving from God was proof of God's love for him. Then I pointed him to the wisdom of God in Jesus Christ through the Holy Spirit.

He inquired how he too could come to have such a relationship with Jesus and personally experience that indescribable love of God.

Over the phone, I read to him Romans 10:9–10, "That if thou shalt confess with thy mouth the Lord Jesus, and shalt believe in thine heart that God hath raised him from the dead, thou shalt be saved. For with the heart man believeth unto righteousness; and with the mouth confession is made unto salvation."

When I was done, I asked if he believed in his heart what the Scripture had said. He said, "Yes, I do."

Then I said, "Now what you need to do is confess with your mouth that Jesus is Lord. Give him your sin, and then take Jesus's righteousness as your own. You'll become a new creation and begin a real relationship with Jesus."

What happened next was miraculous!

I had been praying for my father and the rest of my family members since I had gotten saved. This miracle was sixteen years in the making. Now was God's appointed time.

My dad was in Kampala, Uganda, and I was in Denver, Colorado, in the United States. Despite the distance between us, I led my dad to the Lord over the phone as He surrendered his heart and life over to Jesus.

My father, like many people now and those back in biblical days, believed because of what he had seen Jesus do in my life over the years and the prophetic ministry of Jesus's love he was experiencing through our conversations.

Six months after my father accepted Christ as his Lord and Savior, he had a physical illness that required hip surgery. The procedure went well, but later, my dad died from an infection he had acquired from the operation.

I miss my dad greatly, but I'm comforted by knowing that I will see him again in heaven. What a loving God we serve.

Join me in the next chapter as I describe the power of God.

What Is the Power of God?

IN THE FALL OF 1987, I finally discovered the power of God as the one thing I desperately needed in my life. But then I wondered what the power of God was. Is it something that any believer like myself could have? And if I could, how can I get it? What does it look like? How do I know if I received it?

These were just some of the questions I had. So, I started a journey of discovery that would mark the beginning of living a supernatural life.

For the next twelve months, I immersed myself in a study of the Bible, focusing on the power of God and the anointing. After about a month of asking those at my church for a Nave's Topical Bible, I found somebody with one, and he let me borrow it for a while.

I wrote out every Scripture—from the beginning of the Book of Genesis to the end of the Book of Revelation—on blank sheets of papers that I stapled together. As I studied these Scriptures, I made a note beside each verse with the insight or understanding that I would receive. My goal in this study was to discover what God said about His supernatural power or anointing so that I could effectively seek it and walk in it daily.

The following is some of what I learned:

WHAT IS THE ANOINTING?

According to *Strong's Concordance*, "Mashach" is the Hebrew word for anoint and means "to rub in, to pour over." It is where we get the noun "messiah." Jesus, the High Priest of the house of God, the Church, is God's anointed. He is the Messiah, and "messiah" is derived from the Hebrew word for anointed—"Christ." Also, "Christ" is derived from the Greek verb "chrio," which is where we get the noun "Christos." Christos is translated "to anoint," which means "to smear or to spread over."

According to the *Webster's Revised Unabridged Dictionary*, "to anoint" means the procedure of rubbing or smearing a person or a thing with oil for healing or setting apart for service. When you accepted Christ as your Lord and Savior, you were spread with the very anointing of God. To anoint is to apply oil, to pour oil upon as a sacred rite, especially for consecration. As part of God's family, you now have God's marking for all to know to whom you belong. That's why when we receive Christ, we are set apart, and the Bible calls us "believers, the called-out ones." We're not only "called out," but we are also anointed, consecrated into the family and the ministry of God.

EVERY CHRISTIAN IS ANOINTED

Firstly, I discovered that every Christian is anointed and sealed at salvation with the power of God according to 2 Corinthians 1:21-22, 5:5. When you become a child of God by taking Jesus Christ into your heart, Father God marks you as His child with His anointing—the salvation or leper's anointing. He pours into you His precious Holy Spirit, and you are anointed. From that moment onward, you belong to His family.

As a result of the new-birth miracle experience, you received the salvation anointing as a seal that says you belong to God.

JESUS WAS ANOINTED WITH POWER

Secondly, I discovered the secret to Jesus's success—the reality that God had anointed Him with the same Holy Spirit and power that you and I have today. One morning the lights seemed to just come on while reading Acts 10:38: "how God anointed Jesus of Nazareth with the Holy Spirit and with power, who went about doing good and healing all that were oppressed of the devil, for God was with Him." I got it. It was my "aha" moment.

I wondered, *Can it be that simple? Is it possible for me to be anointed? Or is it for a few unique believers with a unique calling from God?*

I continued to dig deeper and found that the power of God was and is always for every follower of Christ.

As you can see from Acts 10:38, God anointed Jesus Christ with the Holy Spirit and power. We as believers follow after Jesus. We see that God was with Jesus through the anointing or the power of God.

Do you want to change your world where you play, where you work, and where you live? Do you desire to fulfill the plan, purpose, and will of God for you? Do you long to break through the barrier to be successful in your Christian walk or ministry? Whatever it is you desire to experience or achieve, you need the power of God. He has called you into His greatness.

In my deep study, I discovered that through the Scripture, the words "anointing, anoint, power" were used synonymously to refer to God's supernatural power or anointing. So, let's look at the meaning of "power" when it comes to Jesus.

WHAT IS POWER?

Jesus was anointed with power. He also promised that His disciples would receive power in Acts 1:8. The Greek expression for power is "dunamis." This is where we get the English word *dynamite*. Dynamite destroys whatever it touches, but not so with God's dynamite power. God's power is much more than dynamite, and yet it's life-giving, reviving, healing, transforming, saving, and a blessing.

Many sources define "dunamis" as divine power, ability, might, strength, force, sway, dominion, miraculous power, mighty works, abundance, workers of miracles, and wealth. As God's sons and daughters, He longs to share His power in full with you and me, but we must first know what God's supernatural power is and then look to Him to give it to us afresh daily.

GOD'S POWER AND ANOINTING

So what is the anointing or the power of God? It is simply the divine enablement for success in Christian life, service, and ministry. Religiosity and legalism are always trying to make man good, holy, and righteous in their strength and effort. However, God has already provided the means for us to be able to live the Christian life that pleases Him and to do the work of ministry effectively. That solution is called the power of God or the anointing.

To have a better understanding of this solution, let us explore different expressions in the Scripture.

1. THE ANOINTING IS THE POWER OF THE HOLY SPIRIT (ACTS 1:8).

Jesus promises that His disciples will receive power. You will receive the miracle power, the dynamite of God, so to speak, to testify about Him with great effects in your life and others. Every time we see healings, miracles, signs, and wonders, that's the Holy Spirit manifesting Himself in power. As a result, you begin to testify. Without the power—the anointing, the Holy Spirit's manifesting Himself in and through the believer—there's no testimony; there's no proof to confirm the Word of God.

2. THE ANOINTING IS ALSO THE POWER OF GOD (PSALM 62:10–11).

Power belongs only to God, and only God can give you His power. You and I have access to that power 24-7 through Jesus Christ.

3. THE POWER OF GOD IS THE RESULT OF GOD'S PRESENCE (EXODUS 33:18–21).

That's why in Luke 24:49, Jesus told the disciples to wait in Jerusalem before talking to people about Him. The early apostles needed to stay in God's presence first. The presence of God is going to impart His power upon you.

As you learn to live in His presence, you discover that the anointing is the fruit of what you get out of it. As you spend more and more time there, the power of God is going to begin to drip in you and through you to others. Why? Because you have been in His presence, which is now producing its fruit as the power of God begins to release its manifestation in your life.

The power then produces the acts of God that follow. The presence of God is always abiding in you, and this power is dynamic.

4. THE POWER OF GOD IS THE MANIFESTATION OF THE GLORY OF GOD (EXODUS 40:34–38).

When the glory of God came down, God began to manifest Himself. "Then the cloud covered the tabernacle of meeting" (Exodus 40:34). There was action. In some versions, it's rendered as the "tabernacle of witness." Why is that? Because it was a place that had proof of God's dynamic works and acts.

Activity was occurring in that tabernacle. God was with His people. The power of God produced visible and tangible acts.

What brought the power was the glory. The glory came down, and then there was activity, a move of God. His glory provided the anointing in the demonstration of power in the tent of witness or meeting.

5. THE ANOINTING IS ALSO THE UNCTION OF GOD (1 JOHN 2:20–27).

Learning the truth and abiding in Christ take the power of God.

6. THE ANOINTING IS THE POWER OF THE MOST HIGH OR THE POWER OF THE HIGHEST (LUKE 1:35).

In Luke 1, a conversation between Mary, the mother of our Lord, and the angel Gabriel took place. We read, "The angel answered, 'The Holy Spirit will come on you and the power of the Most High will overshadow you, so the Holy One to be born will be called the Son of God.'" In the New King James Version, it renders it "the power of

CHAPTER 2: WHAT IS THE POWER OF GOD?

the Most High" as "the power of the Highest." The power of the Most High was required to conceive Jesus into Mary's womb.

7. THE POWER OF GOD IS THE FINGER OF GOD (LUKE 11:20).

How did Jesus cast out demons? By the power of God. So that tells us that the power of God, or the anointing, is the finger of God. That's how the Egyptians described it in Exodus 8:19 when God delivered the children of Israel. It represented the mighty power of the anointing manifesting the miraculous wonders of God.

8. THE POWER OF GOD IS THE OVERFLOW OF CHRIST'S LIFE IN A BELIEVER (JOHN 15:4–5).

When you live a lifestyle of abiding in Christ and Him in you, that union results in the overflow of His life into yours. This overflow releases His power, which now empowers you to bear much fruit.

9. THE POWER OF GOD IS THE SPIRIT WITHOUT MEASURE (JOHN 3:34–35).

You may say, "But Andrew, that was Jesus."

Yes, but remember, we walk in the same class as Jesus because of His finished work of redemption. I know that might be hard to believe for someone. However, we don't have anything we can receive on our own merit, including salvation. We can enjoy God's redemptive blessings by what Jesus has accomplished in our name and in our place on the cross and what the Word of God promises.

If Jesus received the Spirit of God without limit or measure, so can you. I'll show you how you can experience the Spirit without measure in my next book in the series *Catch and Release* the Double Portion.

10. THE POWER OF GOD IS THE HAND OF THE LORD (2 KINGS 3:15–16).

You see, it was after the hand of God that came upon Elisha, meaning it was the anointing or the power of God that came upon him, from which he prophesied.

11. THE POWER OF GOD IS THE POWER OF HIS MIGHT (EPHESIANS 6:10).

By the Spirit of God, Paul admonished and encouraged the church at Ephesus to be strong in the Lord and in the power of His Might or the anointing.

Thirty-three years later, I still refer back to my notes each time God brings to remembrance something I had forgotten or shows me a new truth regarding His power.

I encourage you to get familiar with these expressions because they'll help you understand the power of God better as you use your personal key ring in this book.

Now that you know about the power of God, continue onto the next chapter as I tell you why you need His power and why God desires for all of His children to be anointed and to walk in it daily.

CHAPTER 3

Why You Need the Power of God

TWENTY-THREE YEARS AGO, one of our intercessors in Uganda brought her grandson with epilepsy to my house at four in the morning. He had been convulsing for hours and bit his tongue and was now bleeding in the mouth. They had done everything they knew how.

When I saw the boy, the Holy Spirit simply said, "Just do Mark 6:13." I recalled that Scripture: "And they cast out many demons, and anointed with oil many who were sick, and healed them."

How did the epileptic boy get healed? I will tell you in a moment, but first, let me show you why you need God's power as we see the results it can produce in us, for us, and through us.

THE POWER OF THE ANOINTING

Most of the time when people hear the words "anointing or power of God" or "to be anointed with power," they dismiss it as something available only to those called into the ministry. I believe most people think of ministry merely as a pulpit or missionary work.

For example, a school teacher who is teaching his or her students for the glory of God doesn't see herself as a minister carrying out kingdom ministry in the educational sphere. A stay-at-home mother dedicated to homeschooling or raising her children in the ways of righteousness doesn't consider what she's doing as advancing the Kingdom of God in the family sphere of influence.

But if every member of the body of Christ had a shift in their thinking and how they did things so that it aligned with New Testament Kingdom thinking, they would see themselves as ministers in their given spheres of influence. With that realization, they can look to God for power to impact their lives and their world where God has put them for His glory.

As they carry out their daily lives and occupations unto God, they carry God's presence and power within them wherever they go. They are activated to release life and power in a tangible, life-giving, life-changing way.

At that point, there's no more secular or spiritual. The lives lived and work carried out unto God are sacred and glorify Him, whether in the church, in the home, or in the marketplace.

No more thinking that the professional clergy are the only ones to receive and walk in God's power and miracles while the rest of the Church body is left to go to the few men or women of God to experience this power.

The clergy actually makes up only one percent of the Church, and laypeople make up ninety-nine percent. No wonder the Church is not as effective as it should be. How can the one percent minister effectively to those in the Church and hurting world? That's why I believe God desires each and every one of His children to be fully mobilized, equipped, activated, and empowered to release His unlimited supernatural power daily in their lives and in the world around them.

There are two reasons why the anointing is the most significant need of every believer. The first one is for success in our Christian lives, and the second one is for success in Christian service. Without the anointing, you can't be successful in your life or serving God.

I believe that to get a better understanding of our greatest need as believers, we have to understand why we desperately need the power of God and its resulting miracle blessings in and through our own lives to bless others.

David said, "You anoint my head with oil and my cup overflows" (Psalm 23:5 NIV). Overflows with what? With the fullness of God's life.

Remember, we talked about how the anointing is the overflow of God's presence in you. When you're full of the anointing, you're saturated and filled, and you're overflowing with the very life of God.

I pray you put this in your spirit. You need the anointing more than you'll ever know. Its blessings are endless. We'll address many of them in this chapter.

I encourage you to take inventory as we discuss every resulting blessing of the anointing. Do you have it? If not, do you want it?

At the end of this chapter, we'll identify how you can get any of the blessings you're missing. Let us now go through these results in no particular order.

NINETEEN RESULTS OF HIS POWER IN AND THROUGH OUR LIVES

1. YOU'LL RECEIVE POWER TO WORK MIRACLES.

When the Holy Spirit comes, He imparts His power to work miracles. Jesus couldn't do any wonders until the Spirit anointed Him.

The Bible tells us in Acts 10:38, "How God anointed Jesus of Nazareth with the Holy Ghost and with power: who went about doing good, and healing all that were oppressed of the devil; for God was with him." The anointing of God empowered Him to start working in miracles, signs, and wonders.

People have asked me, "What is the key to miracles, signs, and wonders? Is it great faith? Is it a great prayer life?"

Both faith and a vibrant prayer life are foundational, and they'll lead you into power. When Jesus came to Earth, He was 100 percent God. He put on flesh and blood and was subject to human limitations like us. He became man in covenant with God. He couldn't accomplish any ministry or His mandate that Father God had sent Him to do here on Earth until power came upon His life.

Likewise, His disciples and witnesses—you and I—must follow His model. We need the anointing so that we can continue to work His miracles, signs, and wonders. We believers can walk in the same anointing of God as Jesus did. That's right. If Jesus received the anointing and was able to work miracles, so can you. The anointing will empower you for a lifestyle of miracles.

I want you to put that into your spirit. It doesn't depend on you; it depends on the mighty working of God.

Mark 6:13 says, "And they cast out many devils, and anointed with oil many that were sick, and healed them."

When the Holy Spirit touches you with the anointing, it brings healing, and it brings the hand of God upon your life for the impossible to become possible.

2. YOU'LL RECEIVE THE POWER FOR MINISTRY.

Both you and I are witnesses for Jesus our Savior. According to Acts 1:8 (NIV), Jesus promised, "But you will receive power when the Holy Spirit comes on you, and you will be My witnesses, (proof producers) in Jerusalem, in all Judea, Samaria, to the ends of the world" (my emphasis was inserted).

Jesus promised His Church the power to witness through the Holy Spirit. That anointing was going to enable us to produce the evidence of who Jesus was and what He had done for you and me. Only when we plug into the anointing of the Holy Spirit can we begin to access the fullness of redemption's essences in Jesus's name.

Acts 4:33 (NIV) says, "With great power, the apostles continued to testify to the resurrection of the Lord Jesus. And God's grace was so powerfully at work in them all." Remember, with great power, the power of the anointing, they continued to testify because they were empowered, they got anointed. If you desire to be a witness, to be a proof producer, to be effective and fruitful in the ministry where God has placed you, you need the anointing.

It doesn't matter whether you work in the children's ministry, minister on the streets, teach a Bible study, or run a business. Why? The anointing makes our knowledge and our faith fruitful and productive.

Also, God's anointing releases the power of the Holy Spirit and is the only way we're going to overcome the power of Satan in our lives and others.

3. YOU'LL RECEIVE BOLDNESS TO PREACH THE GOSPEL.

"That couldn't have been you. You were bold and confident. Where did you get that courage? It was like you were a different person."

These were some of the sentiments expressed by my friends and those who knew me after they saw me preach on the streets in public for the first time.

I couldn't believe it either, but it was happening. I couldn't explain it. I didn't know from where that courage to talk to strangers had come. Prior to experiencing the baptism in the Holy Spirit, I was so shy to the point that when family members would come to visit, I'd hide in the bedroom.

As I learned more about the work of the Holy Spirit, I then realized that when I was filled with Him, He anointed me with power and gave me courage. My newfound boldness was the result of His work in me and was not my doing. The Holy Spirit gives boldness to every believer who dares to look to Him for it.

The same boldness came upon the apostles when they were told to stop preaching in the name of Jesus and threatened with prison. They went and prayed. When the power of God came upon them, they were bold in their witness, and they continued to speak the Word of God with more audacity.

> And when they prayed, the place where they were assembled together was shaken. And they were filled with the Holy Spirit, and they spoke the Word of God with boldness (Acts 4:31).

The power of God is tangible, it's visible, you can feel it, and you can touch it. I'm so excited for you because I believe God wants you to be the nation shaker, the community shaker of your environment, a transformer, even a reformer of the sphere where He has put you. He wants you to make an impact in your world, and God's power gives you the courage to be that person.

4. YOU'LL RECEIVE POWER FOR VIBRANT AND PREVAILING PRAYER.

Acts 4:24 says that when the apostles were told not to preach, they moved in prevailing prayer. That prayer released the earth-shaking power of the Holy Spirit. He not only came upon them but also upon the environment where they were. As a result, they were empowered to go forward in boldness.

The power of God drives you into the deeper chambers of prayer. You might be struggling with your prayer life right now, but when the anointing of God comes upon you, it brings you to your knees. The Spirit of God is the Spirit of grace and supplication. (See Zechariah 12:10, Ephesians 6:18, Philippians 4:6, and Acts 1:14.)

He leads you into the supplications of God, into the intercession of God, into the weeping, the crying, and the groanings of God. He leads you to pray the will of God. He ignites your heart with a passion for prayer like you have never experienced.

If you desire to deepen your prayer life, seek to be full of the Spirit of grace and supplication, He will anoint you with His power for an authentic and vibrant prayer life.

5. YOU'LL EXPERIENCE GREAT GRACE UPON YOUR LIFE AND YOUR WORK.

Acts 4:33 tells us, "And with great power, the apostles gave witness to the resurrection of the Lord and great grace was upon them all."

When you walk in God's power, you access a greater measure of God's grace. When God anoints you, there is great grace for you because the anointing is for a reason, and it carries a responsibility.

When God gives you His power, He also gives you the grace in all its manifestations to accomplish the purpose of the anointing in your own life and in the lives of others. Because of the anointing, the apostles enjoyed a great measure of God's grace upon their lives and their work, and so can you.

6. You'll live a generous and self-sacrificial life.

The early Church believers encountered the anointing, and it radically changed their perspective of many things, including money and possessions.

> For there was not a needy person among them, for all who were owners of land or houses would sell them and bring the proceeds of the sales and lay them at the apostles' feet, and they would be distributed to each as any had need (Acts 4:34–35 NIV).

As a result of God's power, they were selfless. They lived surrendered, generous, and giving lives, not just of themselves but with their possessions too. God's anointing is going to work that reality in our lives as we allow Him to anoint us and transform us from the inside out.

7. The anointing will give the evidence that God is with you.

We read in Acts 10:38, "How God anointed Jesus of Nazareth with the Holy Ghost and with power: who went about doing good, and healing all that were oppressed of the devil; for God was with him."

How will the world know that God is with us? It's because we carry the miracle-working power of the Holy Spirit's anointing in and upon our lives. That's why the devil can't touch the anointed; he can't defeat you. He knows what the Word says: "Touch not my anointed, do no harm to my prophets." (See 1 Chronicles 16:22 and Psalm 105:15.)

Now, that doesn't mean the devil isn't going to try. But through God's power, you are victorious over his works and schemes against you at every turn.

When the power comes upon you, it marks you, and it sets you apart. That's what it means to be anointed. You are set apart for God, set apart for His purpose, for His will, for His destiny, for His desires in the earth to come to pass in your life and in the lives of others through you. The anointing is going to produce that evidence that God is with you.

8. YOU'LL RECEIVE HEALING IN YOUR BODY.

Where the anointing is applied, it always releases healing. In Mark 6:13 (NASB), we read, "And they were casting out many demons and were anointing with oil many sick people and healing them."

But you have the Anointed One and His anointing living within you, and that anointing heals you. Earlier, we discovered that to anoint is to rub in or to smear. When God anoints you, He spreads the oil of His anointing on you, but He also rubs it into your life, your heart, your mind, and into your whole being. You are saturated, and you are soaked in the anointing. All you need to do now is learn how to access the healing, the power, the blessing of that anointing in your life.

Later on, I'll show you how to minister healing and deliverance to yourself and others through that anointing.

9. YOU'LL HAVE MORE JOY THAN EVERYBODY ELSE.

Joy and happiness are really inside jobs. The anointing is going to break the barriers and remove all hindrances to the pleasure of the Lord, who is your strength. (See Nehemiah 8:10.)

The anointing destroys everything that's contrary to that inward work of grace, of peace in your life so that you can live a joyous experience that God has freely given you through Jesus Christ. The author of Hebrews tells us that through the Holy Spirit, "You have loved righteousness and hated wickedness; therefore God, your God, has set you above your companions by anointing you with the oil of joy" (Hebrews 1:9 NIV).

We believers should be the happiest, most joyous people on the planet. Why? Because God has anointed us with the oil of joy. The joy of the Lord is a result of God's power in our lives.

The Bible tells us that the joy of the Lord is our strength. Yes, it is our strength, and that joy is a result of the Spirit's power working in our lives and producing that miracle of joy that surpasses all understanding.

10. YOU'LL RECEIVE SPIRITUAL INSIGHT AND SIGHT— DISCERNMENT AND PERCEPTION.

Through the anointing, you receive spiritual insight and vision as your spiritual eyes are opened. Suddenly, the scales on your eyes fall off because divine power has touched you. Now you see Jesus in all His glory.

> "I counsel you . . . anoint your eyes with eye salve, that you may see" (Revelation 3:18).

We want to see Jesus lifted up in our lives and in the lives of others. We want to see a great revival. We want to see miracles, signs, and wonders. We want to understand the Word of God. We want to see the oracles of God, the mysteries of God to really know what He's doing?

The power in and upon our lives heals us of spiritual blindness. When the oil of the anointing of the Spirit touches our eyes, it opens them to reality, the reality of what Jesus has done, what is yours in Christ, and what you can be and what you can accomplish in Christ. Suddenly, you obtain this revelation.

As a result of the anointing, you not only have sight, but you have insight into the will, the Word, and the workings of God. You receive discernment (the ability to see into the world of spirits) and perception. You now have the ability to know the secrets of God and of the enemy. You can see what God's Spirit is doing as well as what your enemy Satan is doing.

11. THE ANOINTING DESTROYS THE YOKE OF BONDAGE AND REMOVES BURDENS FROM YOUR LIFE.

What God has done for one, He will do for you. Let us glean that from Isaiah 10:27 that says, "And it shall come to pass in that day, that his burden shall be taken away from off thy shoulder, and his yoke from off thy neck, and the yoke shall be destroyed because of the anointing."

The yoke of bondage is destroyed by the anointing. You're reading this book, and perhaps you're going through something. Maybe you're thinking, *I have generational curses; I have issues I can't get over.* What you need is the power of God to touch those specific areas of your life.

To tie that into the above Scripture, your shoulders represent your authority, and your neck represents your life. God promises that the anointing will come. When it does, it will remove burdens from your shoulders. It will take away those weights that are hindering your authority, like fear, doubt, unbelief, and everything else that weighs you down and prevents you from functioning in your full identity and potential in Christ with real authority.

Any yoke of bondage—poverty, sickness, disease—will be dissolved. Some versions say broken, but the correct translation is *dissolved, destroyed, rendered invisible, and rendered unrecognizable.*

That's why I believe we need power more than ever before. I pray that as we talk about these results, you're beginning to get a deeper appreciation, understanding, and hunger for the power of God. When the anointing is on you, you can be and accomplish so much more in your own life and in the lives of others for the glory of God.

12. THE ANOINTING WILL MAKE YOUR FACE SHINE WITH THE GLORY OF GOD.

Oil represents the anointing of the Spirit. The oil makes your face shine. That's why the children of Israel couldn't look upon Moses when he came down from the mountain after he spent forty days and nights in God's presence. It had produced the anointing in his life that caused his face to shine with God's glory.

Psalm 104:15 (NIV) says, "Wine that gladdens human hearts, oil to make their faces shine, and bread that sustains their hearts." The anointing is going to intensify the work and the visibility of the glory of God in your life.

13. GOD'S POWER WILL SUPPLY YOUR NEEDS.

In 2019, God preached to me, saying, "Son, all you need is in the anointing."

For months, I pondered what that meant and looked like. So, I sat at the feet of the Holy Spirit and allowed Him to teach me.

One of the things He revealed to me was the fact that I was to access the provision already provided by God's power. He showed me through Scriptures and taught me how to access divine provision.

This is what He says in 2 Peter 1:3–4 (TLB), "For as you know Him better, He will give you through His great power, everything you need for living a truly good life. He even shares His own glory and His own goodness with you."

His power has given you and me everything we need. The power of God dissolves the yoke.

Now, we'll go through seasons when God is elevating our faith. He's going to allow us to be stretched so that He can enlarge our knowledge of Him.

The key is, God's power will supply your needs. Notice the past tense in 2 Peter 1:3–4 in God's Word: "His divine power *has given* us everything." You see, it's done. It's not something that's *going* to happen; it's *already* happened.

Our job is to know how to access the vast benefits and blessings of His power, and I'm going to show you how.

Your and my needs are met through the anointing of God as He works with us and through us.

> "For the Lord God of Israel says that there will always be plenty of flour and oil left in your containers until the time when the Lord sends rain and the crops grow again!"
>
> So she did as Elijah said, and she and Elijah and her son continued to eat from her supply of flour and oil as long as it was needed. For no matter how much they used, there was always plenty left in the containers, just as the Lord had promised through Elijah! (1 Kings 17:14–16 TLB).

Imagine the prophet Elijah's conversation with the widow and her sons: "Hey, if you can only tap into your anointing and listen to what I'm saying and obey it, you're not going to lack anymore." (See 2 Kings 4:1–6.)

You see, you have the anointing, but you need to activate that anointing to achieve the supply of the Spirit. (See Philippians 1:19.) The widowed woman thought she had nothing except a little oil to pour.

The supply by the Spirit is going to cost you obedience. Like this widow, she had to obey the Word of God through the prophet by acting on the practical instructions he gave her. She had to act on that word and pour that oil.

"Go pour it into the container," he told her.

As she poured the oil, that anointing flowed, and she filled all the containers until she had no more vessels to fill, and the oil stopped. She sold the oil, paid her debts, and she had more than enough left for her and her son to live on. All through the power of God. That's your portion as well.

14. You'll have the power to live a holy life.

We are all commanded to seek holiness and to seek the anointing. Holiness is a work of the Holy Spirit and is also a work of the anointing.

> Let your clothes be white all the time and let not oil be lacking on your head (Ecclesiastes 9:8 NASB).

Holiness and power go hand in hand. Holiness is going to be the work that the glory and power are going to produce in your life. We see that even Jesus was approved with power according to the Spirit of holiness. (See Romans 1:3–4.) God wants to establish us in holiness and righteousness as He did with Israel (Isaiah 54:14).

Walking in righteousness and holiness is a choice we make daily. God has provided us with the ability to achieve such a lifestyle every day through His divine power.

> His divine power has given us everything we need for a godly life through our knowledge of him who called us by his own glory and goodness. Through these he has given

us his very great and precious promises, so that through them you may participate in the divine nature, having escaped the corruption in the world caused by evil desires (2 Peter 1:3–4 NIV).

It's not about trying to master all the godly discipline and character you can in your own strength. All that helps, but His power is what gives us the ability and empowers us for the holy and righteous life.

And by that same mighty power he has given us all the other rich and wonderful blessings he promised; for instance, the promise to save us from the lust and rottenness all around us, and to give us his own character (2 Peter 1:4 TLB).

The life of obedience and surrender can only be done by the power of God. If we can learn how to yield ourselves to it and allow it to work in us and through us, that work of holiness and righteousness will not become a religious ritual, a legalistic process that we go through every day to try to please God. It will keep us from wondering, *I hope I'm good enough. I hope I please God.*

Now we know we're depending on the Holy Spirit. And let me tell you what—the Holy Spirit is going to call you out at every turn if you're messing up because He's your helper. Remember, He's not only a teacher, but He's your guardian.

We rarely talk about Him being our guardian, but in John 14:18, Jesus said, "I'm not going to leave you as an orphan." In other words, He's going to parent us into the lifestyle of God, into the ways of God, if we will let Him.

We have so many character-building seminars, classes, and trainings that we should use, but let us also look to our parent, the Holy

Spirit. Through the Bible, He will help us produce the fruit of the Spirit, also called "character," in our lives.

Remember, the Holy Spirit is also the Spirit of sanctification. (See 2 Thessalonians 2:13 and 1 Peter 1:2.)

The Holy Spirit sanctifies us by His power using the Word—the truth (John 17:17) and the blood of Christ. Our relationship with God becomes so rich and so full because we're not trying to be good. We have the good Spirit of a good God working both to desire and to perform His good pleasures in us. (See Philippians 2:13.)

If we desire to bring pleasure to God, to walk in holiness, righteousness, obedience, faith, and all the virtues that attract the presence and the glory, then we need to seek the anointing.

This should free you from all religious expectations, all of these burdens. If you're one of those who try so hard to please God, you'll never be able to do so until the Holy Spirit works the pleasures of God in you. Don't even try; just stop and say, "Holy Spirit, I throw up my hands, and I ask You to work Your power and impart Your character in me."

The Bible tells us that the same power, the same healing power, the same power that raises the dead, saves sinners, and breaks curses and yokes is also the power of holiness. It's the power of righteousness.

God is going to give you His character through the working of His power. Do you see how glorious, how significant the power of God is to your Christian life? That's why I said earlier in this chapter that you need the anointing, not only to succeed in your calling and service, but to succeed as a Christian.

15. YOU'LL RECEIVE THE FULFILLMENT OF GOD'S PROMISES.

The power of God works to produce the evidence, the fulfillment of what God has promised us, from healing, to setting us apart, to

48

walking in holiness, to the long list of blessings. It's going to work in your life to bring forth the manifestation. That's why it's always linked to God's acts while the glory of God is linked to His person, presence, and attributes.

> And by that same mighty power he has given us all the other rich and wonderful blessings he promised; for instance, the promise to save us from the lust and rottenness all around us, and to give us his own character (2 Peter 1:4 TLB).

The glory of God will transform your heart into His image. That's why it doesn't stir you up; it stills and silences your soul.

But the power of God gets you excited. It changes your actions. Why? Because the power of God is the hand of God, and it's going to work to bring to pass the blessings He has promised you and me.

16. THE POWER OF GOD WILL DESTROY THE YOKE OF DEBT AND LACK IN YOUR LIFE.

In 2 Kings 4:1–7 (NIV), we're told, "The wife of a man from the company of the prophets cried out to Elisha, 'Your servant my husband is dead, and you know that he revered the Lord. But now his creditor is coming to take my two boys as his slaves.'

"Elisha replied to her, 'How can I help you? Tell me, what do you have in your house?'"

Now, watch this. Continuing with verse 2, "'Your servant has nothing there at all,' she said, 'except a small jar of olive oil.'"

Most believers would say, "Oh no, I'm not anointed, so let somebody else pray for me." Whatever you think is your little "except" is exceptional in the hands of God.

In verse 3, "Elisha said, 'Go around and ask all your neighbors for empty jars. Don't ask for just a few. Then go inside and shut the door behind you and your sons. Pour oil into all the jars, and as each is filled, put it to one side.'

"She left him and shut the door behind her and her sons. They brought the jars to her and she kept pouring. When all the jars were full, she said to her son, 'Bring me another one.'

"But he replied, 'There is not a jar left.' Then the oil stopped flowing.

"She went and told the man of God, and he said, 'Go, sell the oil and pay your debts. You and your sons can live on what is left.'"

The key was the oil; it was the anointing.

What do you have? Just a little oil? That oil is enough—that's the oil of salvation. Now, you begin to walk in that relationship with God. Then pursue the experience of the baptism in the Holy Spirit. If you've received that, then my friend, follow the leadership of the Holy Spirit as He gives you wisdom and practical guidance.

Other keys are obedience, surrender, and taking action on the Word of God. In the widow's case, she had to find vessels and pour. Empty vessels are symbolic of people to pour yourself into.

On several occasions in my personal life and ministry when I had financial needs, God would lead me to give to another individual or ministry in need. As I obeyed God's instructions, my needs were miraculously met.

God, through His power, will destroy the yoke of debt and lack in your life as you seek and follow His wisdom, strategy, and practical instructions. He wants you to be debt-free and to have your needs met more than you do. He is that kind of Father. He is good!

17. GOD WILL PROMOTE YOU.

In 1 Peter 5:6 (CEV), we're told, "Be humble in the presence of God's mighty power, and he will honor you when the time comes." He's going to promote you. He's going to elevate you out of obscurity, out of mediocrity, out of where you are right now to His lifestyle and help you attain the achievements you desire.

So how do we humble ourselves? I like the way Bishop David Oyedepo put it in his book *Toward Excellence in Life and Ministry*: "Humility is coming in agreement with the truth." Firstly, come in agreement with Jesus and the Word of God. Secondly, because humility is a choice, we must make the choice to be clothed with humility daily. Like putting on new clothes every day, we need to choose to put on humility through the blood. (See 1 Peter 5:5.)

18. YOU'LL RECEIVE THE POWER TO ACQUIRE WEALTH.

Through His power, God will give you favor, wisdom, and strategy to create wealth to establish His covenant of blessing with Christ Jesus.

> "And you shall remember the Lord your God, for *it is* He who gives you power to get wealth, that He may establish His covenant which He swore to your fathers, as *it is* this day" (Deuteronomy 8:18).

19. YOU'LL RECEIVE THE POWER TO SUSTAIN YOUR RELATIONSHIP WITH GOD UNTIL CHRIST RETURNS.

Matthew 25:1–10 says, "Then the kingdom of heaven shall be likened to ten virgins who took their lamps and went out to meet the bridegroom. Now five of them were wise, and five *were* foolish. Those who *were* foolish took their lamps and took no oil with them, but the wise took oil in their vessels with their lamps. But while the bridegroom was delayed, they all slumbered and slept.

"And at midnight a cry was *heard:* 'Behold, the bridegroom is coming; go out to meet him!' Then all those virgins arose and trimmed their lamps. And the foolish said to the wise, 'Give us *some* of your oil, for our lamps are going out.' But the wise answered, saying, '*No*, lest there should not be enough for us and you; but go rather to those who sell, and buy for yourselves.' And while they went to buy, the bridegroom came, and those who were ready went in with him to the wedding; and the door was shut."

Do we desire to have a red-hot relationship in our daily walk with God until Christ returns? If so, we desperately need to cultivate a lifestyle of power so that our vessels are full of oil. We want to be like the five wise virgins with vessels that were not only full of oil, but they had an excess in case the bridegroom was delayed. Their lamps, which represented their relationship with God, had to be kept ablaze so they could meet the groom when he arrived and enjoy the wedding with Him. Sadly, the foolish wise virgins didn't have enough oil; their vessels couldn't sustain them until the end.

EPILEPSY INSTANTLY HEALED

Now I'll finish the miracle healing story I started telling you at the beginning of this chapter. I anointed our intercessor's sick grandson with anointing oil in the name of Jesus Christ and cast out the epileptic spirit from his life.

When the oil touched him, it communicated the impartation, the transfer of the miracle healing oil of the Holy Spirit upon him. I felt fire in my hand while I prayed for him.

By the time I said, "Amen," the evil spirit left him immediately. The boy woke up and went home with his grandmother, and I went back to sleep. He never had another convulsion ever since then. The miracle healing prayer didn't take hours; it took about three to five minutes. That was it.

His deliverance didn't happen because I was great—quite the contrary. But I know that the Miracle Worker lives in me, and therefore, His supernatural power is also in and upon me all the time. That same miracle-working power lives inside every believer. As a result, miracles will follow you if you believe that Christ is within you and if you're conscious of His abiding presence and power in you.

It doesn't matter whether someone wakes you up at four in the morning for prayer or you're walking on the street and see someone who needs divine help. When you're conscious about God's power upon you, you can begin to produce the evidence anytime.

We have discussed the many results that the power of God will produce in your life. Now, join me in the next section as I reveal to you the many keys on your key ring and explain how to use them.

SECTION II
THE KEY RING

CHAPTER 4

The Blood of Jesus Christ— The Most Powerful of All Keys

"ANDREW, DO YOU KNOW what the devil fears the most?" the audible voice cutting through the silence asked while I lay prostrate on a small mat in the empty bedroom, my head feeling the cold concrete floor underneath it.

I was on a three-day fast, away by myself to seek God's face as I prepared for an upcoming crusade in Mumias, Kenya.

I immediately stopped, and my eyes popped open. *Who is that? I'm here alone. Who's that speaking to me*, I wondered.

I slowly lifted my head from the floor and looked around the room. I didn't see anyone. Only my Bible and a glass of water were in the room with me. I thought, *Ha! That's strange.*

No sooner had I started to pray again than the voice asked the second time, "Andrew, do you know what the devil fears the most?"

I started freaking out inside, knowing there wasn't a soul around for miles. I thought, *This is either God, or I'm losing it. But it has only been a couple of days into my fast.*

I was still new to hearing God's voice, and He had never outright talked to me like that in the past. I didn't think it was the devil because the devil wasn't going to tell me what he feared the most.

I put my head on the Bible and again started to pray. As soon as I uttered a word, the voice from its invisible source asked me a third time, "Andrew, do you know what the devil fears the most?"

At that point, I was reminded of the story of young Samuel when He heard God's voice for the first time. He went to Eli, the high priest, thinking it was Eli talking to him. Eli told him that when God called, he should say, "Speak, Lord, for your servant is listening." (See 1 Samuel 3:8–10.)

So, I responded, "Lord, the devil fears the name of Jesus Christ." Up until that time, I had cast out thousands of demons from people using the name of Jesus.

"Yes, but that's not what he fears the most," He responded.

"Well, he fears the Holy Spirit."

"Yes," He said, "He fears the Holy Spirit, but He's not what the devil fears the most."

I said, "Lord, he fears the Word of God."

"Yes, but it's not what he fears the most."

Then I ran out of answers. "Dear Lord, I don't know. What does that devil fear the most?"

"The devil fears the blood of Jesus Christ the most," He answered.

"Why does he fear the blood the most and not the name of Jesus, the Holy Spirit, or the Word of God?" I asked in curiosity.

In a gentle voice, He explained, "The devil fears the blood because the blood was the price that Jesus paid for you to be reunited with God, to become a son, a friend, an heir of God's, a joint heir with Christ and to be His bride and become the righteousness of God. He fears the blood the most because through Christ's shedding of it, the devil was defeated, and through the blood, you have unlimited access to the throne of God. Because of the blood, the name of Jesus Christ, the Word of God, and the Holy Spirit work based on what Jesus did when He shed His blood."

That afternoon, I had the privilege to listen to the audible voice of God for the first time as He revealed to me the power of the blood of Jesus. Since then, I have witnessed mighty deliverances, healings, and miracles of thousands around the world through the power of the blood of Christ.

Let me illustrate the kingdom key of the blood of Christ further with the creative miracle story of my new liver. In March 2014, God did one of the most potent miracles I have ever witnessed.

My family and I had been in the mission field in Europe. During the previous September, it had rained every day for weeks, causing so much moisture. The condensation created black mold in the closets of our rented house in Sheffield, England. The symptoms first manifested in my wife through sores breaking out on her skin.

We sought medical help, but they couldn't do anything for her other than prescribe a cream to put on her skin. Interestingly, it happened just two weeks after I came back from one of the biggest events of its kind in Europe—the Burning Bush Festival in Romania. At this festival, many people were healed and set free, and many lives were committed to the Lord.

But before going to the event, the Lord had warned me by saying, "The enemy is going to come at you and your family with everything he's got, and when he does, I want you to know that I'm going to be with you, and I'm going to fight for you."

Now my whole family was getting sick.

After seeking medical help and counsel from our spiritual covering, it was apparent we needed to get out of the house and find the right medical care to address the effects of the mold in our bodies. We miraculously canceled the twelve-month lease we had just signed. We gave away all of our stuff to charities except some clothes, family pictures, and books and came back to America to get treatment.

Upon returning, I thought my wife's symptoms seemed to be worse. Her skin was breaking out with more sores, which were now turning into cuts and bleeding.

When the doctor examined her, he said, "Well, since you all were exposed to the same mold, I want you all to get examined."

So, everybody got checked, and I found out I was worse off than my wife. All this time, God was sustaining me because my liver was in terrible condition. My eyes even looked yellowish from the extreme amount of bilirubin in my blood.

(MedlinePlus's article "Bilirubin in Urine" defines bilirubin as ". . . found in bile, a fluid in your liver that helps you digest food. If your liver is healthy, it will remove most of the bilirubin from your body. If your liver is damaged, bilirubin can leak into the blood and urine and cause the eyes to be yellow.")

My liver was now so jacked up and not working the way it was designed. The liver's primary function is to filter the blood to be used in the other parts of the body and detoxify the food we eat from any toxic substances.

The black mold had impacted my liver to the point that it didn't perform these necessary functions. The doctor put me on a detoxification regime and an antifungal diet, but halfway through that, I couldn't tolerate the medication anymore.

My liver couldn't handle all the stuff that was going through it. I couldn't tolerate the medication, so I called the doctor to let him know. He said that if I was feeling that way, then I needed to start reducing the dosage. The reduction of medication had no impact on the way I felt; I wasn't getting any better.

GOD'S CREATIVE MIRACLE STRATEGY

I was very sick and spending most of my time in bed. One evening while I was laying down, gasping for air, barely able to talk to God, I heard the Lord say to me, "Andrew, ask Me how I'm healing you?"

So I asked, "Holy Spirit, how are you healing my family and me?"

As clear as day, I heard the Holy Spirit say, "I want you to do communion. Anoint yourselves with oil and pray." That was God's healing strategy. I asked my wife Mona if we still had communion elements to do communion.

"No," she said. "They've all been used."

We postponed doing what God told us to do for our healing until we bought more communion elements. At that point, I was the only one in the family able to drive, but I couldn't risk it because I was so drowsy and weak and not able to pay attention to the road.

I'll end up in an accident, I thought.

So I delayed doing communion and anointing ourselves with oil, waiting for when I got better to go to the store. Instead, I got worse and worse. I was so sick, I could barely walk. Still, I needed to call my doctor.

I leaned against the wall as I walked down the stairs to the phone. Then I sat on the couch for a few minutes to catch my breath and rest for a bit to muster up enough energy to make it the rest of the way, which to me, seemed like a mile.

When I called the doctor, he said, "You need to stop everything, all of the medication you're taking because your liver is failing. You can't tolerate it. You need to stop."

At this point, I could barely move. Moreover, I was gasping for air, and I could barely walk back to the couch.

As I reached the sofa to sit down, I heard the Holy Spirit say, "Andrew, you have the same access for yourself as you do for everybody else. Now, I want you to use it." This time, He said, "I want you to come through the blood of Jesus into the throne room. Don't ask for healing, but ask Me for a brand-new liver."

I said to my wife, "At this point, it doesn't matter what we use for communion. Unless God does a miracle, I'm dying. Get whatever oil, bread, or cracker you can find. If we don't have juice, get water. We're going to have communion right now. God gave me the instructions three weeks ago, and I've been waiting until after I buy the elements. Right now, we're going to use what we have. It just comes down to us *obeying*."

My wife brought me oil. It wasn't the regular extra virgin anointing oil that we had used. I don't remember if it was sesame oil or almond oil, but it was one of those oils used to cook our Asian dishes. We also didn't use regular crackers either; it was our kids' rice crackers.

My kids, my wife Mona, and I sat together as a family, and we took communion.

We anointed each other with oil, and we prayed. Moreover, I said a simple prayer: "Heavenly Father, I come to You through the blood of Jesus Christ, Your Son, asking You to take out this bad liver and replace it with a brand-spanking new one."

That was my creative miracle prayer word for word. It was short and to the point, but it was a prayer full of faith, accessing it through the blood. The Holy Spirit answers and witnesses with and to the blood of Jesus.

> And there are three that bear witness in earth, the Spirit, and the water, and the blood: and these three agree in one (1 John 5:8).

Where the blood is mentioned, honored, pleaded, and applied, the Spirit of God comes to witness, to give proof or evidence to the finished work of Christ through the blood. Moreover, He releases His miracle-working power.

I had never experienced anything like this before in my own body. Sure, I've seen many miracles while ministering in crusades and services, but I've never been this up close and personal.

I felt movement under my rib cage on my right side where my liver is located. When I looked to see what was happening, I saw something moving through my clothes. The divine operation was taking place. The Holy Spirit was taking out the sick liver and replacing it with a brand-spanking new one. A new one! I didn't feel any pain.

In amazement, I exclaimed, "Oh, look, Mona, look."

About an hour later, I was finally able to stand up and walk to the refrigerator to get a drink. Lo and behold, it was like I had never been sick.

I want to help you further establish your confidence and faith in the blood of Jesus Christ our Lord. So before I finish this story, let me answer some questions that people frequently ask:

☞ What is applying, sprinkling, or pleading the blood?

The life of Jesus is in His blood. We apply the blood of Jesus Christ by pleading, speaking, honoring, sprinkling, declaring, and singing the blood of Jesus in faith.

☞ Why do we use or apply the blood?

Here are a few Scriptures to rest our faith on and inform our application:

A. The blood speaks both to God and the devil.

and to Jesus, the Mediator of a new covenant [uniting God and man], and to the sprinkled blood, which speaks [of mercy], a better *and* nobler *and* more gracious message than *the blood* of Abel [which cried out for vengeance] (Hebrews 12:24 AMP).

B. We overcome the devil through the blood.

And they overcame him by the blood of the Lamb, and by the word of their testimony . . . (Revelation 12:11).

C. The blood witnesses with the Spirit and the water of the Word on Earth.

For there are three that bear witness in heaven: the Father, the Word, and the Holy Spirit; and these three are one. And there are three that bear witness on earth: the Spirit, the water, and the blood; and these three agree as one (1 John 5:7–8).

D. Access God's throne and heaven's kingdom realities on Earth.

And so, dear brothers, now we may walk right into the very Holy of Holies, where God is, because of the blood of Jesus. This is the fresh, new, life-giving way that Christ has opened up for us by tearing the curtain—his human body—to let us into the holy presence of God (Hebrews 10:19–20 TLB).

and once for all took blood into that inner room, the Holy of Holies, and sprinkled it on the mercy seat; but it was not the blood of goats and calves. No, he took his own blood, and with it he, by himself, made sure of our eternal salvation (Hebrews 9:12 TLB).

whom God displayed publicly [before the eyes of the world] as a [life-giving] sacrifice of atonement *and* reconciliation (propitiation) by His blood [to be received] through faith . . . (Romans 3:25 AMP).

E. **We have redemption and forgiveness of our sins.**
In Him we have redemption through His blood, the forgiveness of sins, according to the riches of His grace (Ephesians 1:7).

And according to the law almost all things are purified with blood, and without shedding of blood there is no remission (Hebrews 9:22).

F. **We can access the blessings of the everlasting covenant in Christ.**
And now may the God of peace, who brought again from the dead our Lord Jesus, equip you with all you need for doing his will. May he who became the great Shepherd of the sheep by an everlasting agreement between God and you, signed with his blood, produce in you through the power of Christ all that is pleasing to him (Hebrews 13:20–21 TLB).

When we use the blood of Jesus, we're involving the life of the triune God into our lives, worship, situation, circumstances, and prayers. We're reminding God that we're trusting in His love and mercy to save and deliver us according to the finish work of Jesus Christ that He did in our name and in our place. We're declaring to Satan that *in Christ*, we defeated him and that he cannot touch us as long as we're under the blood of Jesus. We're also reminding ourselves of the foundation of our confidence in Christ.

⌐ As New Testament believers, is the blood for today?

Yes, it is for today. Here is the command of the old contract:

For the LORD will pass through to strike the Egyptians; and when He sees the blood on the lintel and on the two doorposts, the LORD will pass over the door and not allow the destroyer to come into your houses to strike you. <u>And you shall observe this thing (the sprinkling of blood) as an ordinance for you and your sons forever</u> (Exodus 12:23–24).

Here's why we use the blood as part of the new contract through Christ:

You [believers], like living stones, are being built up into a spiritual house for a holy *and* dedicated priesthood, to offer spiritual sacrifices [that are] acceptable *and* pleasing to God through Jesus Christ (1 Peter 2:5 AMP).

HOW TO RELEASE THE POWER OF THE BLOOD IN YOUR LIFE

You release the power of God in and through the blood by speaking, singing, declaring, receiving, acknowledging, honoring, and trusting the blood of Jesus to affect your sick body, marriage, finances, family, relationships, ministry, etc. There is no right or wrong way of using the blood. The only problem is that there is very little teaching and preaching on the blood today. Therefore, not many believers know the power of the blood. Those few who do, don't use it enough.

WHEN AND HOW TO USE THE BLOOD

In the Old Testament, Israelites sprinkled the physical blood of animals for atonement of their sins and for protection. But as the New Testament priests serving under our High Priest Jesus, we may now sprinkle His blood for forgiveness, salvation, redemption, healing, protection, and victory!

Every situation where you sense you're under the attack of Satan or need special protection, breakthrough, victory, or miracle, that is the time to plead the blood of Jesus.

We take the blood in the spiritual realm and speak it, which is a form of intercessory prayer in songs, decrees, and petitions. When the Israelites sprinkled blood in Egypt, it brought deliverance to their households. When Rahab used the bloodline token, it brought deliverance to her. As mentioned in the last paragraph, the Old Testament high priests sprinkled animal blood for forgiveness of their sins; however, we offer spiritual sacrifices when we use the blood or any other kingdom key according to 1 Peter 2:5 (AMP):

> You [believers], like living stones, are being built up into a spiritual house for a holy *and* dedicated priesthood, to offer spiritual sacrifices [that are] acceptable *and* pleasing to God through Jesus Christ.

Now let me share the rest of my miracle story of receiving my new liver. I was full of vigor and energy; I was a new person. I called the doctor the next day and scheduled a follow-up appointment.

When I walked into the room where the doctor was waiting for me, he stared at me with a mixture of puzzlement, disbelief, and amazement on his face. After several moments of silence, he asked in a soft voice, "What happened? What did you do?"

After I shared with him the details, he shook his head in disbelief, but he knew we were believers. "Whatever you did," he said, "keep doing it because it's working."

I had been on the verge of death, and now I was very much alive! He continued his examination of me and studied my eyes. "Wow, your eyes are perfect!" He checked my liver strength through muscle tests. It was perfect. No further tests were necessary. My liver was like that of a brand-new healthy baby. It was miraculous!

That was six years ago, and I am still going strong and am healthy today.

NOTHING BUT THE BLOOD

It was all through the blood of Jesus Christ.

I wanted to share this miracle with you to illustrate the blood's power. You too can release and experience the wonders of God by your faith as you use the kingdom power key of the blood of Jesus to access heaven and its realities in your life daily.

Remember, all the power keys in your hands work and are useful because of the blood of Jesus. Of all the power tools at our disposal, none opens up heaven like the blood.

At my darkest moment, the Holy Spirit brought me back to this truth. He said, "Andrew, you have the same confidence and access for yourself as you have for everybody else when you minister to them. Now, come through the blood and receive."

I encourage you to take to heart this kingdom key in your hands and begin to use it with faith to unlock heaven on Earth. It's like putting a hammer in your hand to drive a nail into a piece of wood, and you believe the hammer can do that job. You may not be good at swinging so that you can drive the nail straight, but you know the tool in your hand can do it. You may need to learn to hit the nail on the head, but you have no doubt about the tool's efficacy. So it is with the blood or any other tool we're talking about in this book.

Do you need a miracle? Alternatively, do you need a breakthrough, a victory, or need a supernatural touch of God on your life, marriage, children, business, or whatever else you desire. Use the blood. Access your healing, your breakthrough, whatever it is you need. God can do it through the blood.

The Holy Spirit will always produce evidence of the blood. Why? Because it was the price that Jesus paid for your redemption and mine.

Every time we approach the throne, enter through the blood. God can't hold back His promises. He grants us what has already been paid for by the blood. When we understand and unlock the power of and in the blood, then we can release God's supernatural works daily.

The revelation of the blood of Jesus Christ, that it's what the devil fears the most, opened a wealth of power in my life. It will do the same for you. Use it to defeat him and his works of wickedness, torment, and affliction in your life and that of others' daily.

Now that you understand the importance of the blood of Jesus and the power it gives us in our life, let's continue to the next chapter as I discuss the Holy Spirit key.

CHAPTER 5
The Holy Spirit Key

"I HATE TO TELL YOU THIS, although you're so dynamic, you'll never be able to preach again or travel and stand to minister for as many hours as you did before the accident," my neuropsychologist explained after testing me, reviewing reports from other medical providers, and watching one of my preaching videos.

Here's the back story: In December 2001, I was involved in a car accident that left me with a concussion, torn rotator cuff in my left shoulder, damaged vision so that my eyes couldn't move together, dizziness, and loss of balance and memory. In the months that followed, I was sent to different physicians and specialists including the above neuropsychologist who examined me, and then one of the best neurologists in Denver to treat my short- and long-term memory loss. I received vision therapy so I that I could see and read again without strain and pain. Additionally, I saw a surgeon to repair my rotator cuff and went to physical therapy to help me get over dizziness and loss of balance.

My schedule for the next two years consisted of almost-daily doctor and therapist appointments. So when the doctor gave me his bad news, I was discouraged and disappointed. I had put in all the work, keeping my doctors' appointments, doing my exercise homework, and attending every therapy session. I was expecting to hear, "You're getting better, and soon you'll be back to doing what you love to do."

For a moment, I believed the doctor's report. On the drive home, I began to think of what I could do for a new career. How can I still help and make an impact in people's lives? I wondered, *What can I do that doesn't involve travelling, standing on a stage, or speaking like before?*

The doctor had given me his professional advice. It was meant to be my reality and for me to accept so that I could create a new life with limitation, pain, and disability.

That same evening in prayer, I simply asked, "Father, the doctors have concluded that I will never preach, travel, and speak again. But what do You say? Are You done with me in this kind of ministry? Father, I will accept whatever path You have for me. I just want to know what Your report says."

In a still small voice, I heard Him say, "Son, you're healed, and you will continue to do the work of the ministry I've commissioned you to do. You have the Miracle Worker, the Holy Spirit, and His power in you. Now, go and minister that power to others. As you minister to them, you will see that the same power that's flowing through you for their healing is also healing you."

I had cancelled all ministry engagements, but after I heard God's report and direction, I acted immediately. Some pastors in West Virginia and I arranged a weekend meeting of miracles and power.

I flew from Colorado to West Virginia a day early so that I could rest a bit from the long trip and before the meeting. However, the moment I stepped up to minister, it was as if nothing was wrong. I preached a message on repentance and revival. The power of God was so awesome that when I called people to come forward and re-pent wholly to Christ, many did, but some stood up and walked out of the service.

I didn't know what was happening. *Did I offend them?* I wondered. But there was no time to dwell on that.

The ones at the altar were sobbing, pouring out their hearts to the Lord. Broken limbs were healed in the crowd. Tumors disappeared.

Suddenly, the people who had left during the altar call came back into the sanctuary carrying cartoons of alcohol, vodka, and other hard liquors; crack pipes; and boxes of cigarettes. They all laid them on the altar and cried out to God for forgiveness.

God was doing a massive work of spiritual cleansing in individuals as well as in the church. I was told that some of the folks at the altar who had brought these items were leaders in that church.

We had three amazing nights of salvations, miracles, healing, spiritual cleansing, and transformation of a church and community through my vessel. As the mighty power flowed through me to heal, revive, and transform hearts of those in attendance, it was also healing me.

When I went back to my hotel room, I realized I was feeling about 50 percent better. But more healing was on the way . . .

THE POWER OF THE HOLY SPIRIT WITHIN

The Holy Spirit, the Miracle Worker, had been activated in that meeting to produce miracles. In Galatians 3:5, Apostle Paul says, "I ask you again, does God give you the power of the Holy Spirit and work miracles among you as a result of your trying to obey the Jewish laws? No, of course not. It is when you believe in Christ and fully trust him" (TLB).

God works miracles through the person and power of the Holy Spirit, and He is within you waiting for you to access the power He has instilled in you.

> "But when the Holy Spirit has come upon you, you will receive power to testify about Me with great effect to the people in Jerusalem throughout Judea and Samaria, to

the ends of the Earth about my death and resurrection"
(Acts 1:8 TLB).

Whether you and I admit it or not, our greatest need is the power
of the Holy Spirit. It's available to each and every follower of Christ.
This power is not mere energy or force; It's a person. All we need to do
is to know Him as the source of power and how to access His indwelling power in us to touch our lives daily.

One time when the Lord talked to me about knowing the Spirit,
He said, "To need Him is to want Him. To want Him is to know Him.
To know Him is to love Him. To love Him is to obey Him. To obey
Him is to see Him."

Those simple revelatory words have served me well over the years.
I have put them in front of me for a reminder that unless I need, want,
know, love, and obey the Holy Spirit daily, I can't see Him. We can see
Him when we begin to see His acts of power as He ministers God's
love to us.

". . . This is God's message to Zerubbabel 'Not by might, nor
by power, but by my Spirit, says the Lord Almighty—you
will succeed because of my Spirit, though you are few and
weak'" (Zechariah 4:6 TLB).

Success is by the Spirit as He empowers, leads, and guides you in
every aspect of your life. It's paramount for us to know the Holy Spirit,
to have a relationship with Him, to be baptized in Him, to walk in
unity with Him, and to be able to hear His voice.

THE HEALING JOURNEY CONTINUES

A few weeks after the weekend of miracles and power in West Virginia, I traveled to Seattle, Washington. The pastors and Christian leaders there joined me to do another meeting I called "Three Days of Power."

That first night, I was so drowsy, I could barely stand. I tightly held onto the podium, but the power of God was so strong.

While I spoke, the power of God swept through the auditorium like a mighty wind. When I opened my eyes, I saw people falling down and others getting on their faces as they were being mightily touched by the glory and power of God. I yielded to the Miracle Worker within me to move freely through my vessel.

Mass healings, miracles, signs and wonders, and deliverance began to take place. I was on my feet for about five hours casting out demons, prophesying, and testing people who had been miraculously healed. We had recorded salvations, baptisms in the Holy Spirit, deliverances from demonic possessions and oppressions, healings of the sick, and lukewarm believers who had now been set ablaze for God.

When I left the building at midnight, many people were still on the floor under a heavy touch of God. They couldn't move or get up without falling back down.

About three hours later when the anointing lifted, I could walk without dizziness. I didn't need any more medicine for the different issues I had been dealing with. Now I was 75 percent well but not yet completely healed. As long as I was allowing the Holy Spirit to pour out His anointing through my vessel, that power was also blessing me.

God took me one step at a time, and each step was a miracle. Remember, I had been doing everything I was medically told to do, sitting in my house waiting on the doctors to heal me, but I didn't get well. I had some improvement from the injuries but didn't get my life back until I tapped into the source of power—the Holy Spirit and His power within me.

Now, I'm not saying you shouldn't go to the doctor if you need medical help. What I'm saying is that this was *my* experience. I believe God wanted me to know Him better and learn more ways of how He operates, ways I had never considered or known before.

I ministered to many sick people. Most of the time, they got instant miracles, and I was going through a process for my own healing as well. But I wouldn't have it any other way.

The power of the Holy Spirit was fundamental to my healing. But God wasn't done. He had more to teach me as He used the next key—worship and holy communion—to take me to the next level.

Continue on with me to the next chapter where I will talk about this power-packed key in more detail.

CHAPTER 6

The Worship and Holy Communion Key

THEN A FEW WEEKS PASSED after returning from the Seattle meeting, and I excitedly asked God, "Lord, where do you want me to go next?"

I expected Him to lead me to the next city to minister, but He had a different strategy for my complete healing from my automobile injuries.

"Son, I want you to come away with Me. Remove all distractions and come be in My presence. Worship and have holy communion every day, and I will finish everything that concerns you and heal you completely."

In order to focus on God the way He wanted me to and enjoy my time with Him, I decided to move from Denver, Colorado. I needed to get away from the big city, away from the many things that vied for my attention. So I packed my belongings and moved to a small town where two of my close friends lived.

I told them and those at the church I started attending that I was there to focus on being with God. I wasn't available to minister, not even to lead a Bible study or prayer meeting.

During this time away with God, I would wake up and go to one of the bedrooms that I had converted into my prayer room. I would say, "Holy Spirit, here I am as You instructed me. Lead me now in my worship of Jesus, in communion with You, the Father, and the Son, and in my prayers."

Then I would yield for Him to carry me into the presence of God. I would worship, have communion, read the Word, worship, and pray until I felt the Spirit was done praying through me for that day. My prayer and communion sessions lasted between four to eight hours every day for the next six months.

Then I noticed I didn't have any pain. My memory was restored. Dizziness and drowsiness had gone. My eyes were working together, and I could now read for hours without the strain and headaches I used to get.

Then at the end of my six-month follow-up appointment with my medical provider, the doctor told me he couldn't find anything wrong with me. He asked, "What did you do?"

I told him what I did, and he couldn't believe it except to say it was a pure miracle. He added, "I've never seen anything quite as remarkable as this."

It was so amazing. I didn't do any of the therapies I had done when in Denver. It was all through the Holy Spirit who worked healing in my entire body and soul.

KEYS TO MY HEALING

The Lord started with the Holy Spirit key for my healing, but then He used both worship and holy communion for my complete healing. Worship brings the power or hand of God upon our lives, into our space and position.

> "But now bring me a musician." And it came about while the musician played, that the hand (power) of the Lord came upon Elisha. He said, "Thus says the Lord, 'Make this valley (the Arabah) full of trenches'" (2 Kings 3:15–16 AMP).

Whereas praise focuses on what the Lord has done, worship focuses on who God is. In the above Scripture passage, the musician played, and the power of God was released upon the prophet. He began to prophesy.

Today, the Spirit is not coming upon us for a moment of service. He lives in us. When we exalt God and fix our gaze upon Him in worship, whether it be in song or words of worship, the power of God's Spirit within is released to touch us and others through us.

The time I spent with the Holy Spirit also included having communion with Him. I listened to His heart and His thoughts, His feelings, and His emotions for me. I yielded to Him and asked Him to release His indwelling miracle power within me to permeate my whole being until I was perfectly and completely made whole.

And He did just that.

Now it's your turn. Use the power key of worship and holy communion to connect into the power source within you, and experience the miraculous wonders of God in your life and through you like never before.

EXPERIENCE GOD'S POWER THROUGH WORSHIP

A few years ago, I spoke at a pastor friend's annual conference held just outside of London, England. Just before I got up to speak, I sensed in my spirit that God wanted to do a mighty work in the people's hearts and lives. I perceived that we were to first consecrate ourselves to Him through prayer of repentance.

I also discerned that the people in the audience were looking forward to hearing me speak and not wanting to get into prayer. How do

I shift the atmosphere and the people so that we could get into a time of deep consecration?

I did what Elisha did in 2 Kings 3:15–16 given in the previous section. When he needed the power of God to come upon him to prophesy, he asked for an anointed minstrel or musician to worship.

God had given me a message on holiness, His presence, and His blessings from Psalm 24:3–5. Additionally, I had brought with me a few songs on a jump drive just in case the worship team didn't know the worship songs the Spirit had highlighted to me for the message. I needed the atmosphere to be charged with God's power and the people's focus to be on God and not what I was going to speak.

So, I told the soundman to play the worship track "O God, O God, O God" on the drive and invited the audience to close their eyes and tune their minds and hearts onto Jesus. The worship team didn't know the chorus, so I had everyone listen to it a few times. Then I invited them to sing with me as we repeated that chorus, which was a form of intercessory worship prayer to God.

As we sang the simple but anointed chorus in intercession and repentance, the atmosphere began to change. We sang it again and again. Each time, the presence of God increased and increased and intensified. Suddenly, the hand of God came upon me and the people in the audience. One by one, they began to weep and get on their knees crying out to God for forgiveness of their sins and the sins of their country.

Everything had shifted by worship. That brought into our midst the mighty hand of God and deep conviction that is necessary for true repentance and consecration. For the next half hour, we repented, prayed, and worshipped. God was doing a deep spiritual cleansing of His house and reigniting a new love, fear, and passion for Him.

The audience was multicultural with attendees from all sorts of religious, racial, and cultural backgrounds. For the past twenty years,

I had traveled and ministered in special events, crusades, and conferences in England. Certain races, especially the men, had always seemed to be more reserved in their expression and not hungry or desperate for God. But on this night, the conviction was so strong that even they fell prostrate on their faces and wept like babies before God.

For about fifteen minutes, I spoke from Psalm 24:3–5, careful not to break the flow of the Spirit. Then I invited those who didn't know Jesus as Lord and Savior to receive Him into their hearts. A few Muslims, Hindus, Buddhists, Sikhs, and nonreligious folks, as well as many backsliders, surrendered their lives to Christ. Also, the power of God was so awesome as we ministered to the sick and the oppressed. We witnessed mighty miracles of healing and deliverance.

That's how powerful the kingdom key of worship is for you. I urge you by the grace of God to cultivate a lifestyle of worship with words in Spirit and truth. (See John 4:24.) Worship in music as part of your daily lifestyle so that you can unlock the hand of God upon you.

As for me, I have several playlists for different purposes. For example, I have a worship playlist for when I need to soak in God's presence, to fellowship and worship Him with words of love from my heart. I have another playlist for when I just want to be still and know His voice. These are songs that help me to be one with the Lord in spirit so that my soul is still and quiet within me, allowing my spirit to hear Him.

I have another playlist for when I sense I need to engage in more intense prayer with binding and loosing and making declarations. I have a fourth playlist for when I need to dance before the Lord, praising and thanking Him for what He has done or what I believe He is doing or is going to do.

I have a fifth playlist of songs that evoke the power of God upon me both in my private worship time or in the ministry. I take these playlists with me everywhere I go.

BUILD YOUR WORSHIP PLAYLISTS

What would your worship playlist be? I encourage you to put your favorite worship songs in different playlists so that they are readily accessible to you. When you worship, you can focus on God and not get caught up looking for the songs or changing to a different song. The particular playlist can play over and over until you're done without interrupting your worship and prayer. Today, it's much easier to have your favorite songs with you on your phone, in your car, and on your computer for whenever you need or want them.

Worship unleashed the power of God upon Elisha in 2 Kings 3:15–16, and he prophesied. Find yourself some anointed music, the kind that helps you get deeper into His presence.

At the conference that took place in London, I needed God's power to invade the place and shift the atmosphere. In that particular meeting, the right kingdom key to use was not prayer, praise, binding and loosing, or making declarations. The right key was worship. As a result, the hand of God came upon us. After that, it was so easy to deliver the message that God had given me for the people. That event was just one of many where I've experienced God's power and glory through worship in ministry as well as in my private personal prayer times.

Remember, true worship focuses on God and His heart for us. As we worship Him in the beauty of His holiness, we unlock His presence and consequently, His almighty power for His supernatural.

But praising and thanking God for what He has and is doing has its place as well, so join me in the next chapter as I discuss this powerful key available to you.

CHAPTER 7

The Praise and Thanksgiving Key

"ANDREW, STOP SEARCHING for a house to rent. I have given you a house paid for in full as I promised you eight years ago. Now get ready to move into your new home," the Holy Spirit whispered into my spirit.

This word came to me at the beginning of summer 2016. My wife and I had just received a letter from our landlord telling us that he was putting our rental house on the market for sale. He gave us a choice to buy it from him or vacate the property in sixty days.

We contemplated buying it so that we wouldn't have to go through the hassle of moving, especially with four young children between the ages of one and five years old. But after much thought and prayer, we decided it wasn't the right home for our growing family. Also, we didn't have the cash to pay it off, so we would have to obtain a mortgage, which didn't line up with our plan.

When Mona and I got married in 2009, we sought God's guidance for the purpose of our marriage. In our marriage mission statement, we wrote that we agreed we would never borrow money. We determined we'd be debt free so we'd have the flexibility to get up and go wherever and whenever God sent us without any financial obligation holding us back. Not having the cash to pay for this house in full left us with one option—start looking for another suitable house to rent and move before the sixty days were over.

For two weeks, we searched for and looked at houses, but we couldn't find the right one for our family.

We started to get nervous, wondering, *Are we going to be able to find something here? Do we need to move to a different town?*

Then one morning as I finished praying, the Holy Spirit said, "Get ready to move into your new home." To say I was excited and relieved is a gross understatement.

I asked, "Lord, where is this house? How do I find it or know where it is? What do you want me to do right now?"

"Praise and give thanks," He responded.

EIGHT-YEAR MIRACLE IN THE MAKING

Let me give you a little bit of the back story. In 2008, I had used my life savings to plant a new church in North Dallas.

One evening as I sat in my recliner winding down from the busy day, I wasn't praying. I was resting, and that's when the Holy Spirit asked me, "What do you want me to do for you?"

"Lord, what do you mean?" I responded.

"You obeyed when I asked you to invest your savings in My house, so tell me what you want Me to do for you?"

The question caught me off guard. I thought for a few minutes about what I really needed. "Lord, I want a house fully paid for." I then described the house to the Lord.

"It's done," He said.

From that day on, I was no longer praying for a house but praising and giving thanks for the promised house. Can you imagine for eight years I gave praise and thanks to the Lord for my paid-in-full house?

In 2009, I got married and told my wife about God's promise to fully pay for our house. Several years passed. We had children, and I told them about the house God had given us.

"But, Daddy," they would ask, "where is it?"

"God knows where it is," I assured them. "We just need to praise and thank Him for it. And at the right time, He will show us where it is."

Every day since that moment, we thanked God for our house during our family prayer times.

Our family continued to grow. Now we also needed a minivan. After praying for the minivan a few times, we received assurance in our spirits that the Lord had heard our prayers, and it was a done deal.

For the next two years, we thanked God for our new minivan in addition to our home. At some point, our kids would pray that prayer of thanksgiving without even thinking much about it, saying, "Thank you, Lord, for our house and new minivan." In the natural, however, it seemed as if those promises would never get fulfilled.

THE PROMISE FULFILLED

We continued to praise and give thanks. Two weeks passed by—nothing.

"Are you sure you heard from the Lord?" my wife asked.

"Yes, I did," I answered.

A month went by, and we were still waiting to receive the house. It was coming down to the wire as we neared the two-month deadline to move.

Then early Tuesday morning as I went into the kitchen to make some coffee, I heard my cell phone beep with a voice message. I picked it up from the kitchen counter and listened to it. The caller was Christine, a long-time dear friend. She had left a message the previous evening while I had been in weekly prayer with my ministry team and intercessors, but my cell phone had been turned off.

Christine said, "We've been looking at houses for the past few days, and I would like for you to look at two of those houses to see which one you'd like. I'll take care of it."

My jaw dropped. I listened to the message again to make sure I heard it right. She was going to buy us a home!

Then I hit callback and Christine picked up. She said, "I'm wondering if you have any time to take a look at some houses we've found for you. I'm going to take care of it." She then told me how much she was giving us to purchase the house.

"Sure, I have time," I replied.

After breakfast, my wife met with Christine and the realtor to see the houses. Neither were quite suitable for us, so the search continued.

Mona searched an online website and found a house she liked. After showing it to me the next morning, I set up an appointment with the realtor to see it. Then twenty-four hours later, we learned that the price for it had just dropped $20,000.

A few days later when I walked into that house, I knew it was our home. It had an open kitchen, numerous windows for natural sunlight to stream in, a big backyard for Mona's gardening, and a large open field at the corner of the street where the kids could play. I knew it was the perfect fit for our family.

That afternoon, Mona and the children came by and saw the house. Everyone fell in love with it. We put in an offer to buy the house, and it was accepted. Furthermore, because the price had dropped by $20,000, we were able to use the leftover money that Christine had given us for the house to buy the minivan. The rest, as they say, is history.

Before I finish telling you the story, let me share with you how we receive fulfillment of God's promises, victory, blessings, and miracles through thanksgiving.

> . . . For all things are yours . . . And you *are* Christ's, and Christ *is* God's (1 Corinthians 3:21, 23).

If all things are ours, then how do we begin to access them? By praise and thanksgiving.

Thanksgiving is the outward manifestation of your faith. It's acknowledging you have what you believe even though it hasn't yet manifested. It is the seal of your faith.

When you begin to give thanks, you have now shifted from hope to active faith. Now your prayer has changed. Your vocabulary has changed regarding that need or situation. Now you're acting and speaking as if you have received your desired result in the natural. In thanksgiving, you are now owning your miracle, the promise of God, before it manifests in the physical.

For years, I would tell people in my meetings to start thanking God after I prayed the mass prayer for miracles for them. It didn't matter if they didn't know how to pray. I would tell them to repeat after me, "Thank you, Jesus, for healing me. Thank you, Jesus, for setting me free."

As they did that, suddenly, the crooked leg became straight. The tumor disappeared. Instantly, a miracle happened.

Why? Because they weren't asking anymore; they were receiving. Thanksgiving is receiving. You're taking it, and you're owning that promise. You're owning the anointing, and you are thanking God for the power of the anointing, what it does and will do in your life. You're going to find yourself experiencing that anointing in a tangible way.

THANKSGIVING CAN LEAD TO A MULTIPLICATION OF RESOURCES

How did Jesus multiply fish and bread to feed the multitude? It was through a simple prayer of thanksgiving.

> Jesus then took the barley loaves and the fish and gave thanks to God. He then gave it to the disciples to distribute to the people. Miraculously, the food multiplied, with everyone eating as much as they wanted! (John 6:11 TPT).

God doesn't want us to be anxious for anything. Instead, bring your needs to Him.

> Be anxious for nothing, but in everything by **prayer and** supplication, with **thanksgiving**, let your requests be made known to God; (Philippians 4:6).

DON'T KEEP ASKING

Pray until you receive assurance in your spirit from the Lord regarding your desired miracles. Once you receive that confirmation, stop petitioning prayer and move into praise and thanking prayer. Most of the time, we don't see the manifestation of our desired result because we're still asking for something that God has already given us a long time ago, but we haven't acknowledged it and received it with our faith.

As we finish the story about the manifestation of our miracle home and family minivan, let me point out that it took eight years before the promise of the home was fulfilled. But I never doubted once that God wasn't going to fulfill His promise. I kept my faith focused on the integrity of God by continually praising and thanking Him for that beautiful house. It took two years of daily thanksgiving before our family's minivan manifested. When it came, it was the make and the year we had asked for initially with all the suitable features for our young family.

What are you believing God for? Do you desire to catch and release His supernatural daily? I encourage you to also cultivate a lifestyle of praise and thanksgiving for what God has already done and what you are believing Him to do.

Here is what Paul says: "But thanks *be* to God, who gives us the victory through our Lord Jesus Christ" (1 Corinthians 15:57).

God has already caused you to triumph. Now activate your faith and receive it through praise and thanksgiving.

The Miracle Worker lives inside you.

Join me in the next chapter as I explain the power of the baptism in the Holy Spirit and why you need to use that key to walk in God's supernatural.

CHAPTER 8

The Baptism in the Holy Spirit Key

"I WAS BORN with one foot shorter than the other," John testified at the Ignite Faith Conference in August 2018. "I needed extra support in my shoe to walk without pain. Last year in April, my wife and I attended the Encounter God's Power gathering, and Pastor Andrew released the miracle power of God on the audience in a prayer for healing. I woke up the next morning and found that my foot had grown new tendons, cartilage, and muscles that weren't there before. Now I can stand on both feet, and I don't need the extra padding and support in my shoe."

What did I do for the manifestation of His creative miracle for John? The same thing you're capable of doing. You have the believer's power too, and I'm going to show it to you before I finish John's story.

The principle to experiencing every believer's power is the baptism in the Holy Spirit with fire and power. When we got saved, we experienced the indwelling of the Spirit. The Bible tells us that as an earnest guarantee for salvation, God put His Spirit into our hearts. (See 2 Corinthians 1:21.)

But when we experience the baptism in the Holy Spirit and God's fire and power that comes with it, we're empowered to walk in the believer's signs and wonders as witnesses for Christ. (See Acts 2:1–4.) The baptism in the Holy Spirit is vital for our success and effectiveness in our Christian lives and service.

"You shall receive power when the Holy Spirit has come
upon you, and you shall be witnesses to Me in Jerusalem,
in all Judea, and Samaria, and to the end of the earth"
(Acts 1:8).

If you have not yet experienced this blessing in your life, you can
access it today by following the "Steps to Being Baptized in the Holy
Spirit" given later on in this chapter.

So, what are we witnessing as promised in the above Scripture?
We're testifying to the life, suffering, death, burial, resurrection, and
ascension of Jesus Christ. That's why the power of God is upon you
to testify—to produce results in your own life as well as in others.
The primary purpose of that anointing is for you to begin to be
Christ's witness.

What is a witness? According to Merriam-Webster.com, "witness" means one that gives evidence, something serving as evidence or
proof; to see or know by personal presence; to have direct cognizance
of; to bear testimony; to give evidence; to testify. Who is a witness
for Christ?

A witness for Christ is a believer through whom the Holy Spirit
and His power are manifesting, giving proof that Jesus Christ is real,
alive, and present in the now. You don't have to be a pastor, apostle,
prophet, evangelist, or teacher to witness for Christ. The believer's
anointing is to become a priest or minister of God. A minister is any
believer who does any work unto God in the name of the Lord. So, I
use the word "minister" in a broader sense, and I don't limit its meaning
to professional clergy work.

RIVER LEVEL ANOINTING

The river level of anointing is for serving God and is only experienced through the baptism in the Holy Spirit. This level is where we start to conquer demons, where we start to have authority over sickness and disease, and where we start to walk in the power of signs, miracles, and wonders. Now we have more divine power flowing within us and through us, not only to change other people's lives but to also change our lives.

On the last day of the feast, the great day, Jesus stood up and cried out, "If anyone thirsts, let him come to me and drink. Whoever believes in me, as the Scripture has said, 'Out of his heart will flow rivers of living water.'" Now this he said about the Spirit, whom those who believed in him were to receive, for as yet the Spirit had not been given, because Jesus was not yet glorified (John 7:37–39 ESV).

HOW TO RELEASE THE POWER OF THE BAPTISM IN THE HOLY SPIRIT

I strongly believe that God's power is for every believer to enjoy and release daily as part of our everyday walking-around life as promised in Mark 16:17–18:

"And these signs will follow those who believe: In My name they will cast out demons; they will speak with new tongues; they will take up serpents; and if they drink anything deadly, it will by no means hurt them; they will lay hands on the sick, and they will recover."

Jesus promised "these signs" to follow them who believe. In John 7:38, He revealed the key for any believer to walk in signs and wonders: "He who believes in me as the scripture said, out of his heart will flow rivers of living water."

This is every believer's anointing—to live and walk in signs and wonders regardless of one's calling, spiritual gifting, experience, or maturity level. But why have most believers experienced the baptism in the Holy Spirit, and yet they have no power? Let me submit two thoughts for your consideration:

1. Yes, many believers received the baptism in the Holy Spirit, which introduced them to the fire and the power of God, but they didn't cultivate a lifestyle of the anointing to excel in that power. The anointing opens the door into the divine omnipotence of God in and through our lives.

2. The second thought is the lack of activation and releasing of that power within them. I think this is due to the false belief system of many believers that signs are to follow only a few chosen evangelists, apostles, and prophets or those individuals with the special spiritual gifts of faith, healing, or working of miracles. But that's not what Jesus taught. He said the prerequisite is to "believe," which applies to any believer in Christ.

It's true that healing evangelists, apostles, and prophets or those individuals with the special spiritual gifts of faith, healings, or working of miracles have a greater measure of God's anointing and see a greater manifestation of His power through signs and wonders. But that shouldn't stop us from walking in the signs of the believer in our everyday lives.

The key to activating and releasing the river of living water within you is to take action. That's when the power begins to flow and amplify in your life.

Most believers have experienced the baptism in the Holy Spirit, and it has ended there. That's why over time, they're dry, and it's as if they never experienced the power of God. You need to keep flowing in the river.

Jesus calls us saying, ". . . If any man thirst, let him come unto me, and drink. He that believeth on me, as the scripture hath said, out of his belly shall flow rivers of living water" (John 7:37–38).

Take some simple steps. Begin to release that power over yourself and others. Share the gospel with somebody, and lay hands on the sick. Minister freedom to someone tormented by the devil. Encourage someone discouraged and so on. (I will show you how later on in other chapters.)

Obedience always brings blessings. When you act in faith to the promises in the Word of God, this river begins to enlarge. During dry and harsh situations, the river level will go down. When you're battling the enemies of God in your life and in the lives of others, the levels go down. When you're active and thirsty, then you continually go to Jesus and drink. This is not a one-time thing that we do. This is a daily coming and getting filled with the anointing of the Spirit.

That's why I'm encouraging and teaching you to cultivate a lifestyle of power, not a one-time experience. As you do, you'll begin to see God bring about the reality of commands like "Heal the sick, raise the dead, cure those with leprosy, and cast out demons. Give as freely as you have received!" (Matthew 10:8 TLB).

The Holy Spirit comes and imparts power. That's the power for us to become priests, to serve. We begin to serve in the household of God. We begin to be part of sharing the good news and discipling the nations with the gospel of the Kingdom of God in one way or the other. We begin to take the action necessary that carries us from spectator to participant in God's mission.

THE FULLNESS OF THE HOLY SPIRIT

The baptism in the Holy Spirit introduced me to the unlimited power of God, but unleashing my burning desire helped me to increase and maintain the flow of that power. Here is a story of when God's people unleashed their desire for the Holy Spirit and His power and what happened as a result.

It was a hot summer evening in Sheffield, England, in 2013. My family and I had just relocated from Timisoara, Romania, where we had been living since September 2010. For almost three years, we had been ministering across Romania as well as other European countries.

Our main focus was community transformation, revival, and spiritual awakening in these countries. They had once been Christian but were now more secular than they had ever been.

I traveled, teaching and preaching the principles of awakening, revival, and reformation in churches, at conferences, festivals, and rallies in big tents. I preached the gospel of the kingdom in power, miracles, signs, wonders, and the prophetic in festivals and open-air gatherings held outside in soccer fields, playgrounds, and large open grounds.

One evening while praying in preparation for the upcoming Burning Bush Festival in Ponoare, Romania, the Lord spoke to me, repeatedly saying, "Andrew, your greatest need is the fullness of the Holy Spirit and His firepower in your life. It is also the greatest need of each and every one of my children. Now go and help them know their greatest need; I stand ready to meet their need."

Just before we broke for lunch on the first day of the festival, I preached about having a burning hunger for the Holy Spirit. Then I led the packed tent of over 5,000 hungry people in prayer for God to awaken and ignite a fresh desire for the Holy Spirit, His power, and His work in us.

The power of God was so strong that afternoon. The Spirit ignited faith and hunger in people's lives in preparation for the rest of the festival.

One of the ministers, Evangelist Charles Nzekwe, was standing on the platform with me. Afterward, he came to me and said, "I felt the platform shake when you released the power of God. It felt like an earthquake. I have never experienced anything like that."

When the afternoon session resumed after lunch, everything had shifted. The power of God was lingering in that tent. One speaker after another was being led to minister differently from what they had prepared to do before they came.

As they yielded and obeyed the leading of the Spirit, the power of God intensified to the point that the speaker would stop speaking and call all the ministers to start praying for people. We went down from the platform and began to minister to them. God healed the sick, set the captives free, and performed so many other miraculous works.

I prayed for a ten-year-old deaf and mute girl, and she was instantly healed. While I was testing her, another mother brought her eleven-year-old deaf and dumb girl. I prayed for her, and she too was instantly healed.

These are just two of the hundreds of miracles, signs, and wonders that took place that first day. At this point, it didn't matter who was praying. The miraculous happened everywhere in that tent.

UNLEASH YOUR DESIRE

But that mighty move of God in the story above began with His people having a burning desire for His power that's always present. Most of the time, though, no one is pulling on it by faith.

Remember the story in Luke 5:17–20 where Jesus was teaching, and God's power was present to heal. A paralyzed man with faith and desire was lowered through the roof by his friends and put before Jesus, and a healing miracle happened to him instantly. All who didn't have the desire before then were amazed.

Anything that is worth having is worth desiring, and God talks to us a lot in His Word about desire. May these promises from God's Word serve as a reminder to you that God rewards desire.

"Blessed are those who hunger and thirst for righteousness,
for they will be filled" (Matthew 5:6 NIV).

You can swap the word "hunger" or "thirst" for "desire." Blessed are those who not only desire, but have a burning desire for righteousness, for the Holy Spirit, for His anointing.

What the wicked dreads will come upon him, but the desire
of the righteous will be granted (Proverbs 10:24 ESV).

Dear friend, if you desire the anointing on your life, God's Word says that He will grant that desire.

Delight yourself in the Lord, and he will give you the desires
of your heart (Psalm 37:4 ESV).

God wants to impart His desires in your heart so that you desire what He desires for you. God wants you to have a burning desire for Him, for the blessings of redemption, for the Holy Spirit, for His Word, for a deeper, intimate relationship with Him. He wants you to be on fire because dear friend, you can't truly seek Him (or anything else for that matter) until you desire to burn with the fullness of God's life and God's power.

James 4:2 tells us that you do not have because you do not ask God. In other words, James is saying, "You do not ask because you do not have a desire." When you desire something, you go after it. When you desire the power of God, you seek it.

Do you want to walk in God's supernatural power daily? Then desire it. Ask God for a hunger and thirst that only He can satisfy.

CLAIM, RELEASE, AND RECEIVE GOD'S DESIRE FOR YOU

During one of the sessions, the director of the Burning Bush Festival in Romania turned to me with a smile. "None of this is planned," he said. "You started the unexpected move of the Spirit this afternoon. We praise God for the powerful anointing in this place."

For the next five days, we witnessed one miracle after another, including salvation, deliverance from demonic strongholds and curses, and bondages broken. I was told that we had over 16,000 people in attendance plus over two-million people who watched the festival on live television and through a livestream. Over 2,500 gave their lives to Jesus for the first time, and several hundred healings and deliverances were recorded. It took a whole day to hear all the testimonies from people.

At the end of the festival, the organizers told me that this festival was the most successful and powerful they had ever had in all the years they've been conducting that annual event. Everyone agreed that the success was due to the mighty move of the power of God. I'm sharing this story to emphasize that it's always not by might nor by power but by the power of the Spirit (Zechariah 4:6).

Without the power of the Holy Spirit, there could be no spiritual revivals, transformations, or awakenings for many of the communities we were dealing with, yet they desperately needed it.

This Holy Spirit power is readily available to each and every follower of Christ. All we need to do is to know Him, the source of power, and we will be endued with power daily. But it all starts with having a burning desire and unleashing your desire in prayer and action.

So, I strongly encourage you to start claiming, releasing, and receiving God's desire for you. When you do, the Holy Spirit goes to work in your heart, mind, and life. He starts to remove all that hinders your deep desire for what God wants for you in all things. You may pray something like this:

Dear Lord, fill me with Your desires until they are actualized in my life and regarding all things. Flame Your desire in my heart, soul, and whole being for Your power. In Jesus's mighty name.

Focus your desire in your petition and become more specific about what you're asking. (See Chapter 12 "The Praying with God Key.") Let your desire be focused in your prayers and your prayer focused on the object of that desire. Then watch what God does.

A CREATIVE MIRACLE HAPPENS

When John, the man I talked about earlier in this chapter, came to our Encounter God's Power meeting, he and his wife sat in the back and listened as I taught on the power of the blood of Jesus Christ.

After my teaching, I invited everyone to stand up as the worship team sang, "Oh, the Blood of Jesus." I told the audience to get ready for God to touch them and to focus their eyes on Jesus and have faith in Him and His finished work of redemption through the blood.

After we sang this song a few times, I invited everyone who was sick or needed a touch from God, including those watching the meeting by television, to put their hands where the sickness, disease, or pain was. I told the people that I wasn't going to personally lay hands on them but that I was going to pray a prayer of faith to release God's power through the blood.

As I prayed, I first applied the blood on the audience, and then I released the miracle-working power of the Spirit upon them. As I finished praying, the miracles started taking place.

I asked everyone who needed God's touch to check themselves or attempt to do some type of activity they weren't able to do before I prayed. Then we started hearing testimonies from some of the people God had just delivered.

I get praise reports like John's, from people who have experienced God's miracle-working power on the streets, in stores, at Bible studies, in church services, and at gospel crusades.

How did our friend John receive his creative miracle? I didn't do anything special for the manifestation of power other than applying the blood and releasing the power of God, which any Christian can do as they apply their faith. This is the same power that every follower of Christ who is baptized in the Holy Spirit has received according to the promise of Jesus in Acts 1:8.

This is every believer's power to start serving the Lord. We go from being churchgoers and good Christians to walking in power.

We become priests unto God, capable of taking authority over His enemies in our lives and in the lives of others. We become life changers and transformers!

STEPS TO BEING BAPTIZED IN THE HOLY SPIRIT

It was a rainy day in January 1986, a few days after accepting Jesus into my heart to be my Lord and Savior. My heart was overflowing with praise, songs of love to God, and an unspeakable zest for life. It seemed as though I just got born again, and I was!

I was a new believer, and I didn't know anything about how to pray to experience the baptism in the Holy Spirit. I knew the power of the blood because my mother used to talk a lot about the blood of Jesus Christ. As a matter of fact, we never went anywhere without her pleading the blood of Jesus over us kids.

Then I received the gift of the baptism in the Holy Spirit through the blood. I'll share with you more on how I experienced it, but first, let me tell you about the steps of faith in receiving the baptism in the Holy Spirit:

STEP 1: REPENT.

Now for a believer, our sins were washed away the day we confessed Jesus as our Lord and Savior and invited Him to come to make His home in our hearts. We then repented of those works of the flesh, habits, and negative character traits that hindered the move and work of the Holy Spirit in our lives.

And Peter said to them, "Repent [change your old way of thinking, turn from your sinful ways, accept and follow Jesus as the Messiah] and be baptized, each of you, in the name of Jesus Christ because of the forgiveness of your sins; and you will receive the gift of the Holy Spirit. For the promise [of the Holy Spirit] is for you and your children and for all who are far away [including the Gentiles], as many as the Lord our God calls to Himself" (Acts 2:38–39 AMP).

Peter was talking to nonbelievers. That's why he told them to first "repent." Even for us, we can approach God through repentance and ask Him to cleanse us of all that blocks our vessel so that the Holy Spirit will have a free flow in our lives. The promise of the Holy Spirit and His power is for you and your children and for all who are far away, including the Gentiles, as many as the Lord our God calls to himself.

The gift of the Holy Spirit is not for a few. Any believer in Christ can experience this wonderful gift, having access to Him in Christ Jesus as part of our redemptive blessings.

We now know what we repent of, but *how* do we repent? We're not necessarily focusing on sins, but we are focusing on consecration. One way we can repent includes the washing of our feet, which is when we plead the blood of Jesus to cleanse our lives from sin and be consecrated to God. John 13:9–11 (AMP) will help us understand this consecration:

Simon Peter said to Him, "Lord, [in that case, wash] not only my feet, but also my hands and my head!" Jesus said to him, "Anyone who has bathed needs only to wash his feet, and is completely clean. And you [My disciples] are clean, but not all *of you.*" For He knew who was going to betray Him; for that reason He said, "Not all of you are clean."

You are being set apart through the blood of Jesus for the glory of God to be filled with the power of God. You wash with the blood to welcome the Holy Spirit and to be accepted and feel at home in your vessel.

If you've been walking in wicked ways, yes, go ahead, repent and receive God's forgiveness from your sins. However, in John 13:10, Jesus is saying to those who have accepted Him into their lives, "… He who is bathed needs only to wash his feet …" In other words, if you've been bathed in the blood of Jesus, you have accepted Him. You only need to wash your feet.

What does that mean? Your feet represent your walk or standing with God. They are the only part of your body that touches the earth, meaning the ground, which is symbolic of the world.

Let's return to John 13:10 above and then complete it in the Amplified Bible:

> Jesus said to him, "Anyone who has bathed needs only to wash his feet, and is completely clean. And you [My disciples] are clean, but not all *of you.*"

Judas was having issues involving the lust of the flesh and the darkness in his heart. That's why Jesus said, "… not all of you are clean."

Now remember, Judas was a disciple. He was already following and serving Jesus, but his walk still needed further consecration. That's why as New Testament believers, we can wash our feet with the blood every day, receiving consecration through sanctification.

When we walk in this world, things of this world can attach themselves to us. That's why we wash all the dirt, filth, and mud of this world off of our feet with the shed blood of Jesus. Our walk with Him can then be continuously uninterrupted and kept clean so that we can know His fullness in our everyday lives.

Knowing the power of the blood of Christ is so paramount for us as believers. Being able to understand what the power of His blood can do for you, in you, and through you changes your life forever. Then there is no more shame and no more guilt as you approach the throne of God because you are entering through the blood.

STEP 2: SURRENDER ABSOLUTELY ALL INWARD SELF TO GOD.

What do you surrender to God? You put your heart, your mind, your will, your emotions, your conscious, subconscious, and your body at God's absolute disposal.

What does that mean? Hear the Holy Spirit speaking through the Apostle Paul in Romans 6:13: ". . . But offer yourselves to God [in a decisive act] as those alive [raised] from the dead [to a new life], and your members [all of your abilities—sanctified, set apart] as instruments of righteousness [yielded] to God" (AMP).

Beloved, this verse is what it means to surrender. The great secret of blessedness and power is found in yielding yourself to God completely, always, and entirely, to be His property, for Him to do with you and in you what He wills, for Him to fill you with His Spirit and use you as He wants according to His pleasure and purpose.

To access the great secret of the Holy Spirit and have it come upon your life, you could say something like this in prayer:

Heavenly Father, from now on, I have no will of my own. Your will regarding me in all things be done in me, through me, and

*by me. I put myself unreservedly in Your hands. Now, baptize
me in Your Holy Spirit according to your Word through the shed
blood of Jesus Christ, Your Son. In Jesus's name, Amen.*

You see how simple that was? You can pray that prayer now or
use your own words with faith. God hears you when you ask Him. He
hears your prayer.

STEP 3: ASK.

God will give us what we ask for, so most of the time, we don't have
because we don't ask. Many people don't realize they can simply ask
the Father.

> If you then, though you are evil, know how to give good
> gifts to your children, how much more will your Father
> in heaven give the Holy Spirit to those who ask him!
> (Luke 11:13 NIV).

The Heavenly Father is waiting for you right now to ask Him for
the baptism in the Holy Spirit. If you haven't experienced this incred-
ible blessing, ask now.

> And we are sure of this, that he will listen to us whenever we
> ask him for anything in line with his will (1 John 5:14 TLB).

According to the Scripture, we're sure that God hears our prayer
and grants the answer. I want to give you two principles to help you
ask effectively.

FIRST PRINCIPLE: *Ask with a burning desire:* Whenever you go before God, have that burning desire for the promised blessing. This isn't a religious ritual. You want it, you need it, you crave it, and you desire it with every fiber of your being. Then approach the throne of God boldly through the blood of Jesus, and ask Him. For instance, you must have a burning desire for the baptism in the Holy Spirit upon you. "You do not have because you don't ask" (James 4:2 NIV).

In other words, you ask not because you have no desire. Desire is a big part of your asking. It's your desire that forces you or pushes you to prayer. Passion is the push for accomplishing things. Without hunger, you might have never even gotten out of bed today. But when you have the desire to achieve something, experience something, or receive something, then you do something about it. That's why hunger is so important. Focus your prayer on your desire, or focus your passion in the petition, in the prayer, and in what you're asking.

SECOND PRINCIPLE: *Ask with pure motives*: You must have the right motivation for what you are desiring God to release in your life.

This is what the Spirit says in James 4:1–3 (NIV): "What causes fights and quarrels among you? Don't they come from your desires that battle within you? You desire but do not have, so you kill. You covet but you cannot get what you want, so you quarrel and fight. You do not have because you do not ask God. When you ask, you do not receive, because you ask with wrong motives, that you may spend what you get on your pleasures."

If your desire for the baptism in the Holy Spirit with power is in line with God's will, if your passion is not only to just speak in tongues but to go further and grow in your relationship with God, to know God better, to commune with Him through prayer, through His Word, to bless others through the power of the Holy Spirit, then my friend, you are going to experience this wonderful blessing.

You are bought with a price, (you are actually purchased
with the precious blood of Jesus and made His own) . . .
(1 Corinthians 6:20 AMP).

You are bought with the blood, and that blood has given you access into the wealth and abundance of God's throne and His Kingdom through Jesus Christ. When you approach with the blood, the blood speaks mercy, forgiveness, grace, victory, healing, and power to God. Yet to Satan, the blood of Christ expresses his defeat and fear for all that Christ accomplished in our name and in our place.

Like the Old Testament priests who sprinkled the blood of animals as they approached the throne of God, we also need to approach through the blood because we are New Testament priests in Christ Jesus.

You [believers], like living stones, are being built up into a
spiritual house for a holy *and* dedicated priesthood, to offer
spiritual sacrifices [that are] acceptable *and* pleasing to God
through Jesus Christ (1 Peter 2:5 AMP).

The sprinkling of the blood, the using of the blood, speaking it, declaring it, and honoring it are a spiritual sacrifice that you and I are offering today according to the Scripture. You sprinkle or offer the blood by reverently entering the presence of God with worship, either quietly in your spirit or audibly on your lips. Then you begin to talk to God. You may say something like this:

*Precious Lord Jesus, I approach Your presence through Your shed
blood to receive the gift of the baptism in the Holy Spirit in my
life. Baptize me in the Holy Spirit and power as I honor and*

sprinkle Your precious blood by faith. In your mighty name, Jesus Christ, I pray. Amen.

It's a simple prayer, but be sincere and precise in what you're asking. Then after that, take the precious blood of Jesus by faith and begin to sprinkle it in His presence by repeatedly saying and singing, "The blood of Jesus Christ."

STEP 4: RECEIVE THE BAPTISM IN THE HOLY SPIRIT.

Receiving is by grace through faith. Speak the blood of Jesus in worship, praise, and in prayer. It's like sprinkling a drop of His blood. You can sit down, stand up, or kneel, but don't be rigid or tense. You are accessing one of the many riches of God's grace. You say, "Through the blood, I now receive the baptism in the Holy Spirit."

Begin to speak as the Holy Spirit gives you utterance of what comes to your tongue. Just let it go. Your tongue becomes a faucet that you turn on to allow the river of God within you to begin to flow. If you don't speak, His words can't be heard, and there won't be an outflow of the Spirit from your heart.

Relax and allow the Holy Spirit to touch you. Again, you may stand, sit down, or get on your knees. Get in whatever position you're comfortable in and like the best.

At this point, as you apply these steps, you're experiencing the power of God. Just allow the Holy Spirit to move you, and begin to speak. It's not going to make sense. It's not going to be something you understand. It's not going to be English or any other language that you may usually speak.

You are building yourself up in your most holy faith, praying in the Holy Spirit. (See Jude 1:20.)

STEP 5: LIVE A CONTINUOUS LIFE OF OBEDIENCE.

After receiving the baptism in the Holy Spirit, live a lifestyle of obedience. Jesus Christ identifies obedience as a key to faith and the condition of receiving and retaining the Spirit. You may utter just one syllable, or you could say two or three words; it doesn't matter. The more you speak, the more you intensify the power of God, and your prayer language is going to be powerful.

Everything is going to hinge on your obedience. Are you going to allow the Holy Spirit to use your mouth and your tongue? You do the speaking, but He gives you the utterance. Remember that.

Acts 5:32 says that "We are witnesses of these things, and so is the Holy Spirit, whom God has given to those who obey him (NIV)."

I can't stress enough that obedience is essential not to only receiving the Holy Spirit but to retaining His work and the overflowing of His life and His power in you.

So now, if you desire this blessing, I want you to reread these steps to getting baptized in the Holy Spirit. This second time through, do the steps one-by-one and yield and relax:

1. Repent. Confess habits or negative character traits to God, and wash in the blood.
2. Surrender. Put yourself at God's disposal.
3. Ask. Approach Jesus's presence by honoring and sprinkling His blood before the throne of God.
4. Receive. Speak what the Holy Spirit puts on your tongue.

The baptism in the Holy Spirit is yours. After you have received it, continue to act in obedience to God's leading in your life. You're not going to only have a onetime experience of power, but that power is going to grow and intensify.

Now, find someone else to bless, someone who needs to experience this baptism in the Holy Spirit. Pray with them to experience this blessing.

You're going to see that God is doing wonders in and through you as you allow the Holy Spirit to pour out to others through you.

MY BAPTISM EXPERIENCE

Two days after I accepted Christ as my Lord and Savior, I was singing the blood of Jesus. I was telling Him how much I loved Him and that I wanted to know Him and serve Him. I don't know if it was prayer or fellowship with God, but the more I spoke and declared the blood of Jesus, the more I felt God's love flood my whole being. I knew from deep within that I was loved.

A gentle, warm sensation started to pour onto my head and went through me until I could feel it over my body.

As I continued to say, "The blood of Jesus," suddenly, the power of God hit me. It was sweet but then intensified as if someone had poured hot water over me without burning me. Immediately, I was overcome! Right then and there, I was filled with the Holy Spirit and began to pray in tongues for three and a half hours.

I had no control of my tongue. A torrent of power on the inside of me flowed out. I prayed in tongues, sang in tongues, and worshipped in tongues. It was the most amazing time with God in this newfound walk with Him. I later found out that the Bible calls it the river of living water. (See John 7:37–38.)

I experienced the baptism in the Holy Spirit by honoring the blood. No one prayed for me. I didn't need to fast and pray for days to get it. That day, I discovered a key that I've since used to help thousands of others receive this baptism. I have found it more effective than any other method of approaching or receiving this gift. When you present the blood, the Bible says that the Spirit, the blood, and the water agree as one (1 John 5:8).

The Holy Spirit answers to the blood, and I didn't know it, but I was singing the blood, speaking the blood, declaring the blood, and honoring the blood of Jesus. As a result, the power of God came and took over my life. I have never been the same. I became an intercessor at that very moment.

Now, take the blood of Jesus right now. This is you presenting the price, the blood for you to have access to heaven.

I want you to take the blood of Jesus on your lips and say, "The blood of Jesus" as you ponder what it did for you. Speak the blood with reverence as you honor Jesus for it. In your own words of love, speak with faith the blood of Jesus over you to wash and cleanse you from every sin and from all unrighteousness that grieves Him.

The baptism is a definite work of the Holy Spirit. You can't strive to do it on your own. It's something already provided by our Lord. All can receive it freely by grace through faith.

In the next chapter, I'll tell you about another key on your key ring that's readily available—the Bible.

CHAPTER 9
The Word of God Key

"ANDREW, GIVE THEM THE WORD, and I will confirm it with power, miracles, signs, and wonders," the Lord said to me as I was getting ready to go speak at a conference in South Africa.

When the hosting pastor had invited me to speak, he told me that they wanted to experience the power and work of the Holy Spirit. "Feel free to flow in the gifts and power of the Spirit as the Lord leads you," he said.

So, I knew they were expecting more than a good message, but how did I go about it?

During prayer and preparation for that upcoming conference, I asked, "Lord, I know You love the people coming to the conference and want to speak and touch them. As Your partner in ministry, I put my vessel at Your absolute disposal to work in me, with me, and through me as You please for Your desired results, oh Lord. Wonderful Jesus, show me how You are loving on these people."

Instantly, I heard several Scriptures in my spirit that made up my message. That's when I heard a still small voice say, "Andrew, give them the Word, and I will confirm it with power, miracles, signs, and wonders."

The Word of God shows people the finished work of redemption through the life, suffering, crucifixion, death, burial, resurrection, ascension, and present ministry of Jesus at the right hand of God, and He was going to use His supernatural to validate it. Why give people the Word? Because power is in the Word. It's the sword of the Spirit (Ephesians 6:17). The Word was and is God (John 1:1). The Word is powerful, alive, active, and sharper than any two-edged sword (Hebrew 4:12). The Word is one of the three witnesses on Earth along with the blood and the Spirit (1 John 5:8).

For the next several weeks leading up to the conference, I soaked myself in the Word the Lord had given me for His people. I prayed it, sang it, declared it, read it, and studied it. I yielded to the Spirit not to only make me the vessel for the Word but to become the evidence of the Word I carried.

The day arrived for me to minister. I didn't get to preach per se during the first two services. I only read the Scriptures to the congregation. As I did, God's power fell on the church like rain, starting from the front and rushing to the back.

Suddenly, people got healed across the auditorium. Demons came out of many; blind eyes were opened; and people threw down their walking sticks and crutches, rose out wheelchairs, and walked. Others ran to the front and knelt at the altar to get saved before I could even give the invitation. These were just some of the signs, miracles, and wonders that occurred.

Finally, during the third and final service, I preached the rest of the message for about fifteen minutes. The Holy Spirit confirmed the Word with power, signs, and wonders.

Over and over again, I have witnessed the power of the Word or the gospel in action proving that Jesus is the same yesterday, today, and forever. If we desire to see God at work in our own lives or in the lives of others, we can look to the Bible with full confidence. God is going to confirm His Word with signs and wonders and use our stories and experiences to help build other people's faith in what God can do for them as well. The Spirit is going to witness to the Word with tangible evidence when we receive it, believe it, and act on it.

When we do that, the Spirit goes to work. He takes the Word in our hearts and in our mouths and uses them to fight our enemies in power. The blood has given us the right standing in God's family and household so that we can effectively use the power tool of the Word of God.

We get to know the power of God when we feast on the table of God's Word. It will bring the anointing upon your life, and the Holy Spirit will uncover His anointing through it.

Job 29:6 says, "When I washed my steps with butter, and the rock poured me out rivers of oil;"

When your steps, meaning your walk, your relationship with God, your intimacy with God, are being washed with the Word, He's cleaning you and intensifying your relationship with Him. The Bible tells us that we can also wash our steps, our walk, our feet with butter. Milk in the Scriptures represents the Word, and butter represents the wealth of the Word. The Rock is Jesus Christ pouring out rivers of oil for you.

We experience the anointing through the Word of God because the Holy Spirit is going to take it and anoint us with its power. Then He's going to release the power through the Word, but first, we need to experience its wealth, the butter. Do you want God to anoint you and walk in power? Get into the Word.

Every time we read, study, receive, believe, act, and speak the Word of God, we're washing our feet. We're sucking honey out of the rock and oil (power, anointing) out of the flinty rock.

He made him ride on the high places of the earth, And he did eat the increase of the field; And he made him to suck honey out of the rock, And oil out of the flinty rock; (Deuteronomy 32:13 ASV).

The keyword here is "honey." Honey represents the sweetness, the goodness of God's Word, but He made him suck honey out of the rock. Jesus is the rock of our salvation. As we feast on Him through the Word, on Him who was the Word and became flesh, we are fed and nourished with the sweetness of His goodness and anointed with the oil of His anointing.

You see, when we suck the honey, we enjoy the wealth of God's life in Christ and also get the oil out of the rock. We must be intentional in order for us to suck or nourish well, similar to a baby sucking on a bottle. God wants us to learn to suck honey out of the rock. We do that when we get into God's Word, and the Holy Spirit imparts the anointing.

God is going to cause you to feast on Him. This is the call: "'Whoever is naive or inexperienced, let him turn in here!' As for Him who lacks understanding, she says, 'Come, eat my food And drink the wine I have mixed [and accept my gifts]. Leave [behind] your foolishness [and the foolish] and live, And walk in the way of insight and understanding'" (Proverbs 9:4–6 AMP).

If you're naive, if you lack understanding, experience, and insight, if you're like me and are hungry and thirsty, God says, "Come and feast." The feast is God's. "Come and feast. Have My food, and drink the wine I've mixed."

When you go into the Bible, especially when you dig deep into what Christ has made available, you're going to feast on Him. Then you're going to find out He's feeding you His precious wine. You know the anointing, and you're getting the wealth of His Word into your life. You're going to go from understanding to experiencing.

Also, the Word of God is the sword of the Spirit. The Holy Spirit can't do anything with you if you don't get into the Bible. Period. He can't anoint you. He can't use you because He's always using His Word.

In Psalm 23:5 (NLT), David said, "You prepared this feast for me in the presence of my enemies." Again, this is talking about how the Word of God is a banquet.

Now, watch this. Afterwards in this same Scripture, David said, "You honor me by anointing my head with oil."

As a result of his intimate relationship by feasting through the Word and feeding on God, God anointed him with oil. Then his cup began to overflow with blessings.

In Romans 1:16, Paul tells us that "I am not ashamed of the gospel, (the Word of God) because it is the power of God (my emphasis inserted)."

This Scripture could even read and be interpreted as "it is the anointing of God that brings salvation."

In the Greek and Hebrew Bibles, the word "sozo" or "salvation" encompasses all the works and acts of Christ in redemption. God's Word is the power of God to bring healing from sickness and disease, salvation of our souls, deliverance, freedom, liberty from oppression and depression, and whatever else the enemy might be bringing upon our lives.

The Word of God is the power of God because the Holy Spirit fights with it in your life and through you for everyone who believes. What are you believing God to do in your life, in the lives of your loved ones, in your business, marriage, and other relationships?

Whatever it is, read the Bible and find those promises for your area of need and desire and become one with it. Ask the Holy Spirit to work faith in you for those promises until they are manifested in the natural realm.

If you and I are going to catch and release God's supernatural daily, we need to wash our walk or steps with butter (wealth of the Word) and suck honey out of the flinty rock. That rock will surely pour out to us rivers of oil (power) to manifest kingdom miracles as part of our daily lives. You can pray something like this:

Dear Heavenly Father, in the name of Jesus, I ask and claim the anointing of the Holy Spirit in and through Your Word upon my life so that I may fully know You, experience Your promises, and make You known. In Jesus's name, amen.

In the next chapter, I'll discuss another key for catching and releasing God's supernatural and just how powerful it is—oh, the name of Jesus!

CHAPTER 10

The Name of Jesus Christ Key

"PRAISE GOD! I am the man who got healed of a twisted and crushed disc in my back. I lived with pain for over a decade, just as you described in your prophetic word. I still have a hard time believing that it's true, but it's now six months later, and the pain is gone! It was a real miracle! Like the kind right out of the Bible. I never thought a true miracle would happen to me, but God healed me. As a conservative Christian, I'm usually very skeptical, but this was the real thing. Thank you so very much for being the vessel of God's healing."

This praise report came from a man we'll call Steve. He had attended the Christian NightVision Music Festival 2016, featuring world-renowned Christian recording artists, speakers, and yours truly. Steve had said he didn't come expecting a miracle of healing from the Lord. He and his wife came to enjoy the great praise and worship music together with the tens of thousands of other folks who had gathered to hear an inspiring message from God's Word, engage in good fellowship, and eat good food.

That Friday night during the festival, I was the keynote speaker. I boldly presented the gospel with faith, passion, and power.

As I finished the invitation for salvation, the Lord started giving me words of knowledge for people in the audience of more than 25,000. These words were very descriptive and specific.

One of those words was for Steve, who sat in the middle of the crowd. The Lord said to me, "There is someone here who has been experiencing excruciating pain in their back for the past ten years due to crushed and twisted discs. I want to heal him right now."

I asked the people that if those words described their condition, then wave at me. Because my keynote speech was at night under the lights, I only saw hands wave at me but didn't see their faces clearly.

I asked them to stand up and put their hand where the pain, sickness, or disease was in their body, and I would pray for healing miracles in the name of Jesus. God would then touch them right where they were standing.

Before I finish this story, let me share two thought with you.

RELEASING THE POWER OF HIS NAME

Every Christian around the world uses the name of Jesus Christ in personal and corporate prayer, whether it be for salvation, for healing, deliverance, protection, provision, and the list goes on. Sometimes we're successful in our prayer, and sometimes we're not.

I also understand that there are many factors to answered and unanswered or ineffective prayers. The following are two points in effectively releasing the power of the name:

ONE: WHAT IS THE NAME?

The name is simply the active presence of a person or entity. The name Jesus Christ is the active presence of His person. But to be effective in bringing His active presence or reality into our time and space, here and now, we need to have faith, not only in the person but also in His name. The name of Jesus Christ represents all that Jesus is, has done, and continually does here on Earth as it is in heaven.

Listen to Apostle John in 1 John 5:13–14 (AMP): "These things I have written to you who believe in the name of the Son of God [which represents all that Jesus Christ is and does], so that you will know [with settled and absolute knowledge] that you [already] have eternal life. This is the [remarkable degree of] confidence which we [as believers are entitled to] have before Him: that if we ask anything according to His will, [that is, consistent with His plan and purpose] He hears us."

Using Jesus's name in faith releases His active presence into your midst, your situation, and your need every time. That's why the Bible promises that whoever calls upon the name of the Lord shall be saved. (See Acts 2:21 and Romans 10:13.)

When you call on the name of Jesus, you can expect salvation (sozo) from sin, healing, deliverance, protection, and so forth from the Lord. But you must call in faith so the realities of Jesus's person are at your disposal.

Two: Our Legal Right to Use the Name of Jesus Christ

As a believer in Christ, you've been given a legal right to use the name of Jesus Christ. Let's look at a few Scriptures to remind us of our right and power of His name.

> "But as many as received Him, to them He gave the right to become children of God, to those who believe in His name:" (John 1:12).

"Behold, I give unto you power to tread on serpents and scorpions, and over all the power of the enemy: and nothing shall by any means hurt you" (Luke 10:19).

What power is He talking about? The power of attorney to use His name. Signs and wonders follow those who know the power of the name of Jesus.

"And these signs shall follow them that believe; In my name shall they cast out devils; they shall speak with new tongues; They shall take up serpents; and if they drink any deadly thing, it shall not hurt them; they shall lay hands on the sick, and they shall recover" (Mark 16:17–18).

Whether you're praying for the sick or casting out demons, you're exercising the power of His name. It's all by faith in His name and active presence that's manifested through His name.

Then Jesus came to them and said, "All authority in heaven and on earth has been given to me. Therefore go and make disciples of all nations, baptizing them in the name of the Father and of the Son and of the Holy Spirit, and teaching them to obey everything I have commanded you. And surely I am with you always, to the very end of the age" (Matthew 28:18–20 NIV).

Teaching and baptizing disciples of all nations in the name of the Triune God are not mere religious rituals or exercises. They are to bring the invisible God into our here and now on Earth as He is in heaven. Can you imagine what our world and lives would become if we recovered our right to the name of Jesus and began to use it with reverence, faith, holy fear, and love? Then every mention of the name of Jesus would become a sacred act of worship. We would know the great grace of our Lord Jesus Christ, the unlimited love of God, and the ever-present communion of the Holy Spirit in our lives and work like never before. (See 2 Corinthians 13:14.)

I know from experience that every time I released my faith in the name of Jesus Christ, miracles, signs, and wonders have followed me, my family, and those to whom I minister.

Now, let us finish Steve's miracle healing story in his words: "I've been suffering from lower back pain for many, many years. I don't know quite where it started. It may have been an old football injury from the seventies; I'm not sure. But over the years, it continued to get worse and worse until probably ten to twelve years ago, it started to be painful every single day with the worst [pain occurring] over the past five years. I felt pain through my legs into the night. I couldn't sleep, and it was getting to be really unbearable. The doctor said I had a crushed and twisted herniated disc. The only thing they could do was surgery, which of course, I was trying to avoid. When I went to the night festival, Dr. Andrew described my condition and called for those who needed healing to stand up.

"I'm a conservative Christian, but I went ahead and stood up anyway and prayed a simple prayer. It wasn't anything fancy or special. I just prayed, 'Lord God, if You can heal me, if You're willing to do this and this is Your will, I'll accept it, and I'll take it.' And I did. The next morning, I went to get up out of bed and found myself able to sit up. I didn't have to roll over onto my knees and pull myself up. I sat up and got out of bed. I had had such pain in my lower back that I could hardly bend over and put my socks on in the morning. Sometimes my wife even had to help me. Well, that morning I put my socks on, and there was no pain. I'm going, 'Holy cow, what's this?'

"Then I took my socks off, and I put them back on again. I did it three times. It was unbelievable. Before I received healing, I couldn't pick up a pen off the floor without having to pull myself up by a chair or by a door handle to try to get back upright on my feet again. That pain in my back has never returned, and that was over six months ago. I was living with pain every day, every night, continually for at least five to six years, if not longer. It was a long time, and that pain is gone.

"So I'm here to testify and tell you to tell the world that the healing power of Jesus Christ is real. It happened to me. If it can happen to me, it can happen to you anywhere you are. I'm just here to testify to that and say that it's the real deal. It's not in my head. It's not my imagination. It's not some kind of psychological trick, not when you go six months pain free after having it [the pain] every day for a decade."

Steve's testimony is one of the many people God touched that night at the festival. I have witnessed firsthand the mighty power of the name of Jesus in church services, in hospitals, on the street, in homes, and in mass gospel crusades and festivals like the NightVision Music Festival. I have seen multitudes come to know Jesus as their Lord and Savior, the sick healed, and the captives set free, always in the *name of Jesus Christ*.

The secret to walking in faith, power, and authority of the name of Jesus Christ is the two truths I have shared with you—know what is in the name of Jesus and the legal right you have been given to use it.

Ask the Holy Spirit to renew and ignite passion and faith in the name of Jesus. Lean on the Spirit from this moment on to teach, show, and help you release the active presence of Jesus Christ that's transmitted in His precious holy name.

Now that you understand the power of the name of Jesus, I'll teach you about the power key of hearing the voice of God in the next chapter.

CHAPTER 11

The Ability to Hear God's Voice Key

IT WAS A JOYOUS Tuesday morning on September 9, 2014. My family was basking in the new joy of welcoming its newest member—our third child. The night before was busy as we witnessed this miracle birth.

I had gotten up early as usual to spend time with God before the rest of the family woke up. I didn't go into the prayer room with any particular request but to praise God for giving us a safe birth and a healthy baby.

But God had other things in mind. Perhaps the birth of my son was also a symbol of a new birth in ministry.

As I fellowshipped with the Lord in prayer, He repeatedly said, "Andrew, focus on being My voice, bringing people back to Me, and preparing them for My return. I am coming soon, but the Church and the world are not ready for it. Focus on being My voice."

Even though I kept hearing that statement over and over again, I didn't know exactly what it all meant at that moment. So, I replied, "Lord, show me what it means to be Your voice."

What happened next is nothing short of biblical proportions.

Before I finish this story, let me walk you through the importance of hearing God's voice and how to do it.

HOW GOD SPEAKS

God uses several ways to communicate to us—through prophecies, visions, dreams, impressions, trances, nature, His creations, His written Word (logos), prophetic events, and by directly speaking to us, sometimes in a still small voice whispered into our spiritual ears and at other times, spoken more loudly in an audible voice.

If you're going to do the will of God, first you need to know what it is. God desires to share and reveal His divine will to you in all things, for all things, about all things. But you have to develop your powers of discernment and perception so that you can hear Him when He speaks to you. Even if you think and feel like you can't hear God's voice, the good news is, you can learn.

This chapter is intended to help you get started in learning how to hear God. However, if you already know how to hear God's voice, I pray it helps you go deeper and sharpen your hearing.

FUNDAMENTALS TO HEARING GOD'S VOICE

The following are four fundamentals in no particular order to help you cultivate the lifestyle of power and hearing God's voice all the time:

STRENGTHEN YOUR SPIRIT MAN

The one secret to hearing God's voice is to focus on our trichotomy—spirit, soul, body—in the proper order throughout your day. When your spirit man is stronger than your soul man and your flesh, you can pretty much do anything. You not only hear God's voice, but you're going to walk in power. You're going to walk in authority because the Holy Ghost rules your spirit. As a result, it's stronger and is leading your soul and your body.

Let us see what the Bible says about this in 1 Thessalonians 5:23 (AMP): "Now may the God of peace Himself sanctify you through and through [that is, separate you from profane and vulgar things, make you pure and whole and undamaged—consecrated to Him— set apart for His purpose]; and may your spirit and soul and body be kept complete and [be found] blameless at the coming of our Lord Jesus Christ."

It's always the spirit first, then the soul, and finally the body. When you allow the Holy Spirit to empower your spirit, then the soul (mind, will, and emotions) is under the control of the Spirit of God, who lives in your spirit. Your body follows suit. Your spirit is strengthened against whatever may come up against you because it is being fortified by the Holy Spirit.

Most people are guided by their soul and their body and maybe a little by their spirit. The soul has been corrupted by this world, so your walk will be corrupted, but the Spirit is perfect and gives perfect instruction.

God wants you to live first with a strong spirit man. For instance, your spirit man is like a sumo wrestler—strong. Comparatively speaking, your soul would be like a stick figure in terms of its ability to influence your spirit man.

I'm not saying that God wants you to have a weak mind; quite the contrary. You can have both a strong spirit man and a strong intellectual mind. But He does want you to have a strong spirit empowered by the Spirit of God to influence your soul.

When your spirit has been trained by the Holy Spirit, it's strong, primed like the sumo wrestler, ready to fight whatever the enemy brings.

Now you can effectively align the knowledge, understanding, and intellect of your mind with the truth of God's Kingdom because His Spirit rules and directs you. This decreases your soul's level of influence in terms of determining your responses to life and to hearing God's voice.

Giving your life to Christ means you must yield to the Holy Spirit. God has tasked Him to grow you and shape you into the model of Christ. The flesh becomes under control because the Spirit of God is paramount in your life where He is large, strong, and has free range.

BE FULL OF THE HOLY SPIRIT

We already talked about the source of power and how to receive the baptism in the Holy Spirit if you haven't yet experienced that blessing. You need to be filled with the glory daily, which is the Holy Spirit.

God communicates with your spirit man through the Holy Spirit, not with our soul or flesh. Therefore, it's very crucial for us to able to hear when our spirit is in tune with the Spirit of God.

You will hear God's voice when you seek Him in the depth of your human spirit. That's why it's paramount that you and I have a strong spiritual relationship with God. He connects with us by our spirit by the Holy Spirit. He lives in our spirit man where He overflows in the rest of our being—the soul and the body. Let's learn to seek God with our spirit from Isaiah's prayer in this verse below:

> In the night, my soul longs for you [O Lord], Indeed, my spirit within me seeks You diligently ... (Isaiah 26:9 AMP).

Isaiah is saying, "My soul desires" and the soul is always desiring God, but it's not seeking God. Desire is good because desire pushes you to seek. Yet it is the spirit that's going to seek God.

When you come to a place where you say, "I need to experience the power of God. I need to walk in authority, and I need to hear God's voice," that's the desire.

Then you approach God by the spirit because that's where God is going to meet you.

We hear God's voice in the deep place of our hearts. That's why the Bible tells us to guard our hearts with all diligence because out of it flows the issues of life (Proverbs 4:23).

Deep calls to deep at the [thundering] sound of Your water-falls; All Your breakers and Your waves have rolled over me (Psalm 42:7 AMP).

In this verse, David came into the deep intercourse with the Spirit of God in his heart. He told us that he began to experience the thundering sound of God's waterfalls—"All your breakers,"—the breakers of God, the will of God, the emotions of God, and the thoughts of God. Suddenly, he experienced an overflow.

You're going to experience God in a way you've never done before because now your spirit man is in absolute communion with the Spirit of God. There, the Holy Ghost is imparting and releasing what heaven has for you, my friend. That's why David said "... All Your breakers and Your waves have rolled over me." The NET Bible replaces "rolled over" with "overwhelm," to say, "... waves overwhelm me."

This is the place where your spirit and God's Spirit are one, where you hear God's voice. It's not hard, but it takes learning and practicing, and I'm going to show you how to get there. You must practice it. The more you take action, the faster you'll grow into it.

USE DISCERNMENT

How can you hear God's voice? By discernment.

Discernment is being able to see into the world of spirits or the spiritual world, the invisible world. Sometimes it may involve seeing what God and the enemy are doing.

The Bible talks about the eyes of your understanding, but your spirit man has eyes *and* ears. Like your eyes, you can train your spiritual ears to hear.

> These things we also speak, not in words which man's wisdom teaches but which the Holy Spirit teaches, comparing spiritual things with spiritual. But the natural man does not receive the things of the Spirit of God, for they are foolishness to him; nor can he know *them*, because they are spiritually discerned. But he who is spiritual judges all things, yet he himself is *rightly* judged by no one (1 Corinthians 2:13–15).

This Scripture tells us that the things of the Spirit are spiritually discerned. You hear God's voice by discernment.

My story at the beginning of this chapter about Jesus's visitation and Him telling me to be His voice started with discernment and me responding to that discernment. Then the Spirit took it deeper into a divine visitation that would change and align my life for the second part of ministry.

God is going to give insight, understanding, and revelation by speaking to you in a different language. He's going to open your eyes, and you're going to see things, some you'll like, and some you won't. Your part is to develop your powers of discernment and perception so that you know when He's speaking, how to hear His voice when He does, and then to understand what He's saying to you.

Earlier, we talked about all the ways God speaks to us. God will be talking to you in many ways or with different languages, especially the one He knows you will understand or hear. That's why most people say, "All I do is dream." That's because perhaps it's the only language God can use to get through to you.

Whether it's a divine dream where God is communicating to you, a vision, or a message from your soul, you need to learn to discern if it is indeed God's voice, a dream from the enemy, or something that was simply inspired by eating lots of pizza.

We hear God's voice through the language He's using by discernment.

USE PERCEPTION

You can also hear God's voice by perception:

But immediately, when Jesus perceived in His spirit that they reasoned thus within themselves, He said to them, "Why do you reason about these things in your hearts? Which is easier, to say to the paralytic, '*Your* sins are forgiven you,' or to say, 'Arise, take up your bed and walk?'" (Mark 2:8–9).

Jesus perceived in His spirit what the scribes, or Jewish religious leaders, were thinking. In this Scripture, divine perception is a knowing in your spirit. It's being fully aware, understanding, having revelation, and seeing into the invisible world. Let's read the same verse from the amplified version:

Immediately Jesus, being fully aware [of their hostility] *and* knowing in His spirit that they were thinking this, said to them, "Why are you debating *and* arguing about these things in your hearts? Which is easier, to say to the paralyzed man, 'Your sins are forgiven'; or to say, 'Get up, and pick up your mat and walk'?" (Mark 2:8–9 AMP).

Most people I have talked to say that they can't hear God's voice. But when you have a perceptive knowing in your spirit and you are fully aware of thoughts, feelings, emotions, plans, and ideas, God is talking to you at that moment, and you're hearing His voice through divine perception.

I've been in services or ministering to a person where God used me prophetically. Perhaps He has used you in that way as well. Somebody comes to you and says, "You just read my mail!" It wasn't *you* reading their mail—their thoughts or things happening in their lives. God gave you divine perception.

By the Spirit, you can call out people by their names, their addresses, telephone numbers, places of birth, or some other personal details about them, people you've never met. Acquiring this type of discernment doesn't happen overnight, but you can develop your powers of perception and discernment.

Let me make it clear that our goal in hearing God's voice is not so that we can tell people about the secret or personal details of their lives. It's more about growing your relationship with God as you hear His heart and mind for you and others. When you listen to Him in this manner, you get to know how much He loves you as He shares His will and desires for you.

Sometimes, He'll use you to reveal His love and nature to others by giving you prophetic words for them, words of knowledge or wisdom.

It all comes down to cultivating a lifestyle of hearing His voice so that you can hear Him all the time. I'm serious. You can hear God all the time. You don't have to be in the prayer closet to hear Him. You can hear God while you walk in the crowded street or in quiet place because it is your spirit man that hears Him.

A VISION OF THE FUTURE

Now, let me finish the story I started sharing at the beginning of this chapter, the one about Jesus at my house in September 2014. Remember, while fellowshipping with the Lord in prayer, He repeatedly said, "Andrew focus on being My voice, bringing people back to Me, and preparing them for My return. I am coming soon, but the Church and the world are not ready for it. Focus on being My voice."

So I said, "Lord, show me what it means to be Your voice."

Immediately, I was in the Spirit like John the Revelator experienced in Revelation 4:1–2 and saw the following vision:

A PROPHETIC VISION OF THE END OF THE WORLD AS WE KNOW IT

Suddenly, I saw Jesus standing in front of me. He took me by the hand and began to show me the dramatic end-time events that will happen in America and around the world. We travelled to several cities in various countries on different continents. When He wanted us to go to a city, we would instantly be there.

I saw that what was happening in America was also happening in Africa, Europe, Asia, Latin America, Oceana, and all of the different islands across the globe.

These Were the Events:

WARS

Wars were being fought on every continent. Nation was against other nations with the use of biological and nuclear weapons like in a Hollywood movie, except this was real. Cities were literally being wiped off the face of the earth in a matter of minutes. (See Matthew 24:3–8, Luke 21:8–11, and Mark 13:7.)

PEOPLE VS. PEOPLE

People were fighting against each other.

- Family members shot at each other with guns.
- Fathers and their sons fought as adversaries with swords and knives as they slaughtered each other mercilessly.
- Brothers got into fist fights with brothers, sisters against sisters, and mothers against daughters.

GREAT FALLING AWAY

A significant number of believers turned away from the faith and into the ways and lifestyles of the world. Some of these believers had been servants of God in prominent ministries. (See 2 Thessalonians 2:2–4 and 1 Timothy 4:1–3.)

LOVE OF LAWLESSNESS

People had lost their humaneness and had turned into monsters of iniquity and lawlessness. They loved and enjoyed sin, such as drunkenness, homosexuality, adultery, fornication, uncleanness, lewdness, idolatry, sorcery, hatred, contentions, jealousies, outbursts of wrath, selfish ambitions, dissensions, heresies, envy, murders, revelries, obscene talk, anger, malice, orgies, and drinking parties. (See Galatians 5:19–21,

Colossians 3:5–8, 1 Timothy 1:10, and 1 Peter 4:3.) It was now everyone out for themselves as described in 2 Timothy 3:2–5:

"For men will be lovers of themselves, lovers of money, boasters, proud, blasphemers, disobedient to parents, unthankful, unholy, unloving, unforgiving, slanderers, without self-control, brutal, despisers of good, traitors, headstrong, haughty, lovers of pleasure rather than lovers of God, having a form of godliness but denying its power. And from such people turn away!"

THE SPIRIT OF THE WORLD REIGNED SUPREME

There was no sense of morality and fear of God. Everyone did what seemed right in their own eyes. The spirit of the world had taken over, including many in the body of Christ worldwide. (See Judges 17:5–6 and Judges 21:24–25.)

NO SENSE OF LAW AND ORDER

There was no sense of law and order but rebellious people who were against authority.

MY CURRENT PROPHETIC MANDATE

Jesus and I stood side by side in the midst of this unimaginable and despicable chaos. I was stunned by what I saw.

Holding my hand and with tears in His eyes, He spoke to me, his tone sad yet authoritative. "Call them back to me," He said. "I am coming soon, but My bride and the world are not ready for My return. This is what it means to be My voice, to prepare them for My return, to call My bride to awaken to action."

He pointed out to the sea of people who didn't know Him. "This is what I'm calling you to do when I say, 'Be my voice, bring people back to Me, and prepare My bride for My return.' I am coming soon, and your reward is with Me. Now go, and be My voice. Use every means necessary including mass media. I will be with you."

That wasn't what I had in mind when I went to pray. I came out of my prayer room with a fresh vision, passion, burden, and mandate from God. My wife had just delivered a baby the previous night, so I didn't think it was the time to share such things with her. *She needs to rest*, I thought.

I tried to hold in my emotions, but she could see something had happened. A few days after the encounter, I finally shared what had happened and God's mandate with her. She was excited and responded in agreement with me with a big smile on her face, saying "Yes! I'm with you in whatever the Lord is leading you to do."

I've shared this sacred experience with you to show how this encounter started with a simple word from the Lord—be My voice. But that morning, I wanted to know more. So, I responded to this mandate in a positive way, saying, "Show me what it means to be Your voice." Heaven then opened up to me.

As a result of this visitation and mandate, my passion is to minister God's power through healing and prophetic ministry and to inspire the body of Christ to usher in a great spiritual revival and awakening that will transform lives. I'm burning with God's redemptive love to see souls saved and to prepare the bride of Christ for His return.

On the other hand, if I hadn't responded to that simple word from the Lord, perhaps I would still be doing the old mandate from the old season. As a result, I wouldn't be as effective because I am supposed to be in a new season with a new mandate so that I can be more effective. Since then, the Lord led me to launch a TV program called *Kingdom Come with Andrew Nkoyoyo*.

A few months later, the Lord spoke to me to start a network. Consequently, we launched our online streaming network called *Kingdom Impact Network* (KIN) online with 24-7 live streaming and on-demand channels that are viewed on set-top boxes such as Roku, Apple TV, Amazon Fire TV, Android TV, and podcasts that are watched daily in over 195 countries and counting around the world.

This media outreach is a direct outcome of that word and mandate from God to use every means necessary, including mass media. Our broadcasted online media have gone in countries where I will never be able to hold an open-gospel crusade. I'm training people from all over the world using live webinars and online courses.

Until I received that word from the Lord, I never had any desire to do television or media. I had preached and appeared on many TV and radio networks, but I never dreamed of using media to share the gospel on a regular basis.

The book you are reading is a result of God's mandate. I am on a mission to equip and impact lives both face to face and through all sorts of medium, whether it's broadcasting or publishing.

As I look back over the past thirty years of walking with the Lord, I credit all my success to God's grace and being able to hear His voice. All my failures came from not listening for His voice or failing to obey what He was leading me to do.

Every story in this book, whether it be my personal testimony or from when I ministered to other people, demonstrates the miracle-working power that was released for the manifestation of those miracles and victories. I had not only heard God's voice, but I obeyed it.

I can't stress enough how important it is for you to learn to hear God's voice better. Your miracles, victories, and blessings are connected to His voice. (See Deuteronomy 28:1–14.)

I believe that a new level of power is now in your life as you practice using the keys shared in this chapter. They have helped me cultivate a lifestyle of hearing God's voice all the time, and they will help you too. Just practice them until their realities are actualized in your life by the Holy Spirit.

STEPS TO HEARING GOD SPEAK TO YOU

God is always speaking to you in every situation. It's just that most of the time, we haven't trained our ears to hear His voice because we don't really know how to hear His voice.

The following are several steps you can take right now to learn how to hear God when He is speaking to you.

STEP 1: WASH YOUR EARS SO YOU CAN HEAR WITH THE BLOOD OF CHRIST.

Remember that we have 24-7 access to the throne of God by the blood of Christ. So use it. (More on the power of the blood in Chapter 4 "The Blood of Jesus—The Most Powerful of All Keys.")

When we wash our senses, including our physical and spiritual hearing, all the clogs, hindrances, and barricades are removed. We apply the blood because the Spirit answers to the blood. When you feel like you're all bogged down and you can't hear from God, go to the blood and wash your ears. Honor His blood like Jesus says in John 6:54–58: "Whoever eats My flesh and drinks My blood has eternal life, and I will raise him up at the last day. For My flesh is food indeed, and My blood is drink indeed. He who eats My flesh and drinks My blood abides in Me, and I in him. As the living Father sent Me, and I live because of the Father, so he who feeds on Me will live because of Me. This is the bread which came down from heaven—not as your fathers ate the manna, and are dead. He who eats this bread will live forever."

Wash in the blood. Wash your hearing, your eyes, your whole being, and your whole spirit, soul, mind, and body. Get into the habit of honoring the blood because when you use the blood of Jesus, you're honoring the work of the cross. Receiving His blood and then actually using it makes Jesus so happy.

The Bible tells us that the blood represents His life. The life of the soul is in the blood. ". . . I have given it to you upon the altar . . ." (Leviticus 17:11 NAS). So when you're washing with the blood, you're washing with the very life of Christ. It is paramount. Don't start asking; start with the blood.

Let us see this old contract ritual to further emphasize the washing or applying of the blood on your hearing:

"The priest shall take some of the blood of the guilt offering and put it on the lobe of the right ear of the one to be cleansed . . ." (Leviticus 14:14 AMP).

Now, this is the leper's ritual of cleansing found in Leviticus 14. I want you to read the whole chapter to get the whole context. It is beautiful and unpacks the power of the blood.

The priest takes the blood, the guilt offering of the blood, and puts it on the right ear. Why the ear? Your ears need the touch of the cleansing power of the blood of Jesus Christ. He's the High Priest of the household of God, and He applies that blood. It doesn't matter which terminology you use or how you want to approach this. Just use the blood.

The priest applied the blood on the ears of the one to be cleansed. Today, we're New Testament priests. (See 1 Peter 2:5.) We can apply that blood or directly ask Jesus, the Man who gave His own shed blood, to wash our ears. You may pray something like this:

Lord Jesus, wash my hearing with Your shed blood from all impurities of blockages so that I may hear Your voice, my wonderful Shepherd. In your mighty name, I pray. Amen.

Simple, right? You're asking Jesus to wash you with His blood. Or you may take a direct approach and take authority.

In the name of Jesus Christ, I apply the blood of Jesus Christ on my ears and hearing. I command all barricades to be removed so that I may hear God's voice clearly and consistently. Amen.

You're releasing the power of the blood as you're honoring and applying or sprinkling it on your ears like the priest in the Old Testament did. But you are a new covenant priest with all the priestly rights to apply the blood on yourself and others.

STEP 2: APPLY THE ANOINTING OF THE SPIRIT ON YOUR EARS THROUGH THE BLOOD.

After you've washed your hearing with the blood, now apply the anointing of the Spirit on your ears through the blood. Let's go back to Leviticus 14 because the Old Testament ritual was only a shadow that shows us what we can experience in reality in the New Testament.

The priest shall also take some of the log of oil, and pour it into the palm of his own left hand; and the priest shall dip his right finger in the oil that is in his left palm, and with his finger sprinkle some of the oil seven times before the LORD. Of the rest of the oil which is in his palm, the priest shall put some on the lobe of the right ear of the one to be cleansed, and on the thumb of his right hand, and on the big toe of his right foot, on top of the blood of the guilt offering (Leviticus 14:15–17 AMP).

First, the oil is sprinkled seven times before the Lord. Seven is a biblical number representing spiritual completion or perfection, so it signifies that the anointing you're receiving upon yourself is a complete anointing. It isn't only for some things; it's for all things to destroy all yokes, all bondages. Also, it denotes that the anointing is in the presence of God, and you can have it.

Did you make the connection in the last verse of this passage (Leviticus 14:17), that first, it was the blood and then the oil that was put on the same ear where it was applied: "Of the rest of the oil which is in his palm, the priest shall put some on the lobe of the right ear of the one to be cleansed . . ."

Now the oil or the anointing comes on top of the blood on your ears. Your hearing is washed by the blood.

Beloved, you have removed all barriers. Whatever the enemy has been putting on you, they're all broken, and you can begin to hear at this point.

When I go through this process, it's like heaven is opened to me. I believe it will be opened for you too.

There are a few more steps that I'm going to show you, but at this point, you, my friend, are going to begin to hear God because the blood and the Spirit have destroyed whatever that yoke is. As you practice this step, you may pray something like this:

Lord Jesus, I ask You to anoint my ears and my hearing with oil of the anointing of the Spirit through Your shed blood. Amen.

You see, it's simple, straightforward, but you're sincere. You mean what you say, and you say what you mean and need.

STEP 3: PUT ON THE LORD JESUS CHRIST.

At this point, the enemy comes in doubt and unbelief, and that's why you need to put on the Lord Jesus Christ. You are pressing into a new level of kingdom reality.

But put on the Lord Jesus Christ, and make no provision for the flesh, to gratify its desires (Romans 13:14 ESV).

The devil may begin to bring thoughts into your mind and tell you, "No, you're going to miss it. You can't really hear God's voice."

You see, when you put on the Lord Jesus Christ, you put on His mind, His thoughts, and His life. All of the activities and desires of the flesh are swallowed up. That's why through the Spirit, Paul told us in the above verse to put on the Lord Jesus Christ.

As you're pressing into God, the flesh is always going to come in. That's why I have shown the importance of having a spirit man that needs to be stronger than the soul and the body. If it's not, you'll focus on the works, the activities, the desires of the flesh, and all the lies of the enemy bringing in self-doubt. Or you may believe you're hearing God, but it's not God at this point. Wash with the blood, anoint your ears, and put on the Lord Jesus Christ. Then there's no provision for the flesh. So now, you may pray something like this:

Dear Heavenly Father, clothe me today with the Lord Jesus Christ, Your Son and with Your Spirit. Clothe my soul, body, conscience, and emotions so that I am fully dressed, hidden, and established in Him. In Jesus's mighty name, amen.

As you're putting on Jesus, you're developing a lifestyle of power and empowering your spirit man for discernment and perception from God.

STEP 4: BE ONE WITH THE LORD IN SPIRIT.

You might ask, "What do you mean I'm saved?" Let's look at this verse to help us understand this statement:

> But the one who is united *and* joined to the Lord is one in spirit *with Him* (1 Corinthians 6:17 AMP).

Yes, you are joined to the Lord. You are one in spirit with Him. But if and when the soul man is stronger than your spirit man, a tug-of-war will go on within you.

Yet when you are united and joined with the Lord in spirit, your walk and relationship are very dynamic, vibrant, and life-giving. When your human spirit is married to God's Spirit, it has been blended with His spirit.

I blend my spirit with His every day. It's simple communion that flows out of your relationship with God. The result is a deeper, more meaningful and intimate spiritual union of both of your spirits. At this point, you experience holy silence or stillness in the depth of your soul.

You can hear God's voice clearly as He communicates with your spirit man regardless of where you are and your surroundings. Now pray a prayer of union with the Lord in spirit:

Dear Lord, I surrender my whole spirit to You now. Unite my entire spirit with Yours so that I may be one with You in spirit to hear Your voice today and every day. In Jesus's name, amen.

In your own way, receive this union from the Holy Spirit by faith. Don't let the enemy come between you and the Lord. He's going to try through lies, confusion, or thoughts of unworthiness to convince you that you can't be one with the Lord in spirit. The devil may remind you of your failures and faults from your past and try to convince you that's why you can't have this level of intimacy with the Lord. That's when you wash yourself with the blood and put on the full armor of God and defeat him.

STEP 5: BE STILL AND HEAR GOD'S VOICE.

Be still and know (recognize, understand) that I am God. I will be exalted among the nations! I will be exalted in the earth (Psalm 46:10 AMP).

In the Hebrew Bible, the above Scripture says, "Be still, and know that I am."

We've already talked about how discernment and perception are the results of being in the stillness and the knowing. Your spirit man is going to receive what the Spirit of God is saying at that moment. You know that the Lord is "I AM" in that place of stillness. All of this isn't difficult. You don't have to be hyperspiritual. Just practice the principles I'm showing you. You know the power of the blood.

Almost every story in this book is somehow connected to hearing God's voice and acting in obedience to what He has spoken. The results are miraculous.

In Job 4:16 (TLB), Job said, "I felt the spirit's presence, but couldn't see it standing there. Then out of the dreadful silence came this voice:"

God was speaking to Job, but Job wasn't used to this experience, so he called it a dreadful silence. As you open up to God, you're going to experience this silence. Because you're not used to it either, it will feel strange, like, "Whoa! What is this?" Suddenly, though, you'll be at peace. You're not struggling to touch God or see Him. You're just being there in His presence. The blood has opened the portals of heaven for the anointing and for the Holy Spirit to communicate the wills of the Father and of Jesus to you. As with Job, after experiencing that "dreadful silence," you'll begin to hear God's voice.

> and after the earthquake a fire, *but* the LORD *was* not in
> the fire; and after the fire a still small voice (1 Kings 19:12).

Elijah thought God might be in the earthquake, but He wasn't. Was He in the fire? No, He wasn't. He spoke in a still small voice.

My point is that you may not hear God's voice the way you think you will or want. No, this is a personal experience between you and God. He's going to speak to you according to the language you understand. He's multilingual. He'll speak to you through dreams, visions, prophecies, or by using one of the other languages I mentioned earlier. He wants you to learn how to hear, to discern, and to perceive when He's talking to you.

The point is, God is always talking. It's just that when the soul man is louder and stronger than our spirit man, we can't hear Him.

These are some of the keys that will unlock and unblock your spirit so that there is a free flow of the Holy Spirit, and no barricade between your spirit and God's exists.

STEP 6: BE PRESENT.

Be present in God's presence. Tune your spirit, your soul, and your mind in to what is happening. Ask the Holy Spirit to shut off all other distractions. Be in a quiet place with no disruptions, especially if you're starting out.

As you develop your hearing, you'll be driving in traffic but will still be able to hear God's voice. It'll be like you're listening to a friend. Be ready to hear and to obey immediately. You may want to pray something like this:

> Here I am, Lord. Please speak to me. I'm prepared to listen and obey immediately. Precious Holy Spirit, help me and empower me to hear the voice of the Lord now.

You see, you have made yourself available. You have reached out to your Helper, the Holy Spirit. I encourage you to not be tense or rigid. This isn't a fight. This is communion. You're not trying to contend with heaven.

Jesus said, "My sheep hear my voice, and I know them, and they follow me" (John 10:27). You can hear His voice. You don't have to fast and pray to hear His voice. However, fasting and prayer will always help in your walk with the Lord.

STEP 7: JOURNAL.

Write down everything you sense in your spirit—ideas, thoughts, impressions, words, and Scriptures. Every dream you dream, write it down. Every vision you see, write it down. Every burden, every discomfort, every nudging of the Spirit, write it down. At this point, God is going to begin to speak to you.

Journaling will help you keep track of what came to pass and what didn't. This is very important in measuring your growth in hearing His voice.

In addition, you'll come to know the language that God speaks to you the most and the one you understand the best. Unless you can document them, however, you'll never know whether you're growing and how accurate you are with the message you receive.

STEP 8: ALWAYS INQUIRE.

Let's say you're walking on the street, and you sense something is off or wrong. Stop and inquire of the Lord because in this process, God is going to test you.

Do you really want to know His heart? Do you really want to know what's on His mind, what He thinks and feels? During those moments, you'll begin to develop a deeper level of perception and discernment to what He's doing.

Also, when you get an unusual sense, feeling, or burden, God might be trying to get your attention so that He can reveal something deeper. Are you interested enough to inquire for more? Are you then ready to listen?

Write down or use a digital device like a smartphone to record the time, location, date, and description of what you might be getting from God. Don't yet worry about an interpretation or application of what you see or hear.

When you learn to hear God's voice, He'll teach you how to steward over what He gives you. Also, it provides you with a way to ask Him questions. That's right. God wants you to ask for what you don't understand. So, ask, ask, ask.

Ask for definition, and ask Him to inform you. Ask Him what He loves about you or the people you minister to or encounter. Always start with love. Ask what He means. Ask what He requires from you. This asking or consistent inquiring will get the interpretation and application of what you hear or see in the spirit realm.

STEP 9: FOLLOW GOD'S PEACE IN HIS VOICE.

The test of God's voice is always His peace. When you get that peace with that word, it is from the Lord.

> I am listening carefully to all the Lord is saying—for he speaks peace to his people, his saints, if they will only stop their sinning (Psalm 85:8 TLB).

> At times, God will give you prophetic dreams, visions, or words for yourself or for other people, for a community or nation, and it will overwhelm you and leave you with no peace. Don't throw it out yet. Remember to write it down and inquire of Him. Invite the Holy Spirit to help you process it. Is it a message from God or from the enemy or originating out of your own fears, doubts, or brokenness? Either way, trust the Spirit of truth to reveal the truth from the lies, and you will have God's peace. Follow God's peace.

STEP 10: TEST THE MESSAGE WITH GOD'S WORD.

What is the source of the word or message? Test it, and see if it lines up with God's Word.

> Beloved, do not believe every spirit, but test the spirits, whether they are of God; because many false prophets have gone out into the world (1 John 4:1).

Sometimes you'll get words that don't make sense at first, but don't neglect or ignore them. Journal them, and ask for more information, definition, and clarity. It will be made clear whether it is from the Spirit of God or not.

STEP 11: PRAY IN THE HOLY SPIRIT.

Nothing plugs you into the power source—the Holy Spirit, His gifts, and the workings of God—as praying in the Holy Spirit. I've discovered eighteen benefits or blessings in the Scriptures that come as a result of praying in your prayer language. Two of them are building yourself up while simultaneously praying a perfect prayer according to God's will.

> But you, beloved, building yourselves up on your most holy faith, praying in the Holy Spirit (Jude 1:20).

The Spirit helps you in your weakness of prayer. He knows your desires, longings, and needs, and He knows God's desires, will, and longings for you. He knows what and how to pray even when you don't know what to say. You can rest assured that your prayers are answered (Romans 8:26–27). That's why I can't emphasize enough the importance of praying in the Holy Spirit if you want to be effective, not only in hearing God's voice but in prayer.

In the next chapter, I'll tell you about another powerful key on your key ring and how it will develop a lifestyle of authoritative, effectual, fervent, and prevailing prayer.

CHAPTER 12

The Praying with God Key (to Access Heaven on Earth)

"ANDREW, when the going gets tough, wait upon Me, wait upon Me, wait upon Me," Jesus said when He appeared to me in my living room for the third time, but it wouldn't be the last. (I shared the story of the second occurrence in my book *Working the Works of God*).

It was an encounter and experience like nothing I had ever known or imagined. I'll tell you the rest of this story in a moment, but first let me show you how to pray powerful and effective prayers.

Everything that God has and does is at the command of prayer. The Bible tells us that the effectual fervent prayer of a righteous man avails much (James 5:16). How do we pray effectively? We can learn from the Jesus's model of prayer in Matthew 6:9–13. This model doesn't include spiritual warfare or begging and pleading with God but rather focuses on the worship of God our Father, His Kingdom to come on Earth as it is in heaven, and our position in His Kingdom.

To catch and release God's supernatural daily, we must be anointed afresh daily. That means we boldly stand in Christ as members of God's family and access the power of the Spirit.

There are three levels or realms of prayer as noted in Matthew 7:7–8. It can be broken down as follows:

- Asking prayer is on the ground level or in the outer court prayer realm.

- Knocking prayer is in the inner level or holy place prayer realm.
- Seeking prayer is in the innermost level or Holy of Holies prayer realm.

For the purpose of this chapter, we'll focus on seeking prayer. The following are steps to help you to develop an authoritative and effective daily prayer lifestyle.

STEPS TO DEVELOPING AN AUTHORITATIVE AND EFFECTIVE PRAYER LIFESTYLE

STEP 1: PRAY DAILY FOR A FRESH INFILLING WITH GOD'S POWER.

Every morning when you wake up, in the afternoon, and in the evening, pray to be filled afresh with the Spirit. I want you to see this as a way of life. For example, you eat, drink, and bathe daily, so you should make this part of your routine as well. You want to always be full of the Holy Spirit.

And when they had prayed, the place was shaken where they were assembled together; and they were all filled with the Holy Ghost, and they spake the word of God with boldness (Acts 4:31).

Also, see Acts 4:24, 29–30 TLB.

Note how the apostles were already baptized in the Holy Spirit. You have one baptism in the Holy Spirit, but you have many fillings. Daily, you get refilled and refilled with His Spirt. That's how you not only keep the anointing, but you begin to grow in that anointing on your life.

EXPERIENCE POWER THROUGH SEEKING PRAYER.
Seeking prayer is done by the spirit.

> "Ask *and* keep on asking and it will be given to you; seek *and* keep on seeking and you will find; knock *and* keep on knocking and the door will be opened to you. For everyone who keeps on asking receives, and he who keeps on seeking finds, and to him who keeps on knocking, it will be opened" (Matthew 7:7–8 AMP).

The ask is done on the ground level, but when you're seeking, it's by the Spirit of God leading your spirit. God's Spirit clothes Himself with your spirit. Then He leads you into the prayers of God, the intercession, the supplication of God. Jesus taught that for everyone who keeps on asking, receives; he who keeps on seeking finds; and to him who keeps on knocking, it will be open. So seeking is the most in-depth and authoritative form of prayer in which you and I can participate and how we can get involved with God.

A few years ago, I was on my knees, deep in prayer when the Holy Spirit said to me, "Stop. Go read Ecclesiastes 5:1–3."

I stopped and opened my Bible and started reading those verses. The truth and reality in them hit me like a ton of bricks. "Guard your steps, and focus on what you're doing as you go to the house of God . . ." This was what the Holy Spirit wanted to teach me. ". . . and draw near to listen rather than to offer the [careless or irreverent] sacrifice of fools; for they are too ignorant to know that they are doing evil. Do not be hasty with your mouth [speaking careless words or vows] or impulsive in thought to bring up a matter before God. For God is in heaven and you are on earth; therefore let your words be few. For the dream comes through much effort, and the voice of the fool through many words."

In other words, He's telling us, "I want you to learn to seek." He was teaching me to seek. He was saying, "Andrew, you have a ton of requests to bring before me, but I want you to seek Me. I want you to go in, draw near to Me, be ready to listen rather than offer the careless, irreverent sacrifice of your prayer requests."

Nothing wrong with asking or knocking prayer. They're biblical, but seeking is the most effective and powerful form of prayer. If we're going to ask and knock, then we need to make sure our asking and knocking are according to God's will (John 15:7). Otherwise, our prayers may seem to be unanswered if we're asking God to do what He has already done in the work of redemption or asking Him to do what He has commissioned us to do.

But with seeking prayer, you're not only leaning on your mind but on the Spirit of God who indwells your human spirit. You are listening with your spirit man and praying with the Holy Spirit.

SEEK GOD WITH OUR HUMAN SPIRIT.

By our human spirit, we seek and fellowship with God. When we seek God in the depth of our spirit, the power of God comes upon us.

Isaiah 26:8–9 can help us understand this idea of seeking prayer with our human spirit.

In the path of your judgments, O Lord, we wait for you; your name and remembrance are the desire of our soul. My soul yearns for you in the night; my spirit within me earnestly seeks you … (ESV).

The soul desires and yearns and longs for God, and that's okay, but it does not seek. It is the spirit that seeks God. "My soul yearns for you in the night; my spirit within me earnestly seeks you."

We seek the glory of God with our spirit man, and God communicates with our spirit man. We feel the intense presence of the Holy Spirit in the deep places of our hearts. It's where you and I experience the results that His presence is going to produce within us.

DEEP CALLS UNTO DEEP.

What is this deep calling unto deep that is going on? It is the deep part of the Spirit of God and the deep part of your spirit in deep intercourse.

Deep calls to deep at the [thundering] sound of Your waterfalls; All Your breakers and Your waves have rolled over me (Psalm 42:7 AMP).

As your spirit is encountering the depth of the Spirit of God, His waterfalls, His breakers, and His waves and billows, they begin to roll over you, not over your mind, not over your body, but over your spirit man first. Then and only then will they roll over your mind. You feel them in your body.

The body and soul are going to experience the overflow of what's going on in your spirit man. It's the deep calling unto deep that's taking place between the Spirit of God and your spirit man. As a result, you'll experience the power of the Holy Spirit.

HOW DOES THIS SEEKING HAPPEN?

We seek the Holy Spirit or the glory of God in the stillness and silence of our human spirit because that's where God communicates with us. That's where God is going to talk to us, to speak to us in the depth of our spirit.

Psalm 46:10 (NIV) tells us, "He says, 'Be still and know that I am GOD . . .'"The Hebrew Bible says, "Be still and know that I AM."

The knowing is by the spirit, your spirit knowing the Spirit of God, your spirit knowing God. It's not the intellectual knowing. It's the revelational and experiential knowledge by your spirit.

In the depth of your spirit, you receive revelation and insight. The Spirit is imparting this to you, and you are knowing God. At that moment, whether it's a Scripture, a word, something that God is speaking to you, or an aspect or attribute of God, you get to know Him. But that knowing is by the spirit first—your human spirit.

> "Be silent, everyone, in the presence of the LORD. He is coming out of the holy place where he lives" (Zechariah 2:13 NCV).

God hides Himself in the glory of the Holy Spirit. The presence of the Spirit stills and silences the soul, and His activities release peace into your body. If we want to experience peace, deliverance from depression, anxiety, restlessness, and sleeplessness, we need to encounter the Holy Spirit, who is the glory of God.

When the glory of God fills you, He doesn't stir you up. He doesn't excite you. He quietens your soul because there's an overflow of God's glory in your spirit man. That's why the Bible doesn't say that we're sanctified body, soul, and spirit. It does say that we're sanctified spirit, soul, and body. (See 1 Thessalonians 5:23.) We are spirit beings that have a soul and live in the body. God designed us to live out of the spirit man. When the spirit man is fully filled with the Spirit of God, then we're filled with God, and then there's an overflow effect from the soul to the body.

The result is silence, and not because there's no sound. The silence and the stillness we're talking about is spiritual silence. It's silence of your soul man.

Your soul and the body are at peace, and you're completely yielded to the Lord. My prayer is that you get it because this is what's going to transform your prayer life to one that is authoritative and prevailing and produces God's supernatural.

STEP 2: BE ONE WITH THE LORD IN YOUR SPIRIT.

When you accepted Christ into your life, you united with and joined Him, becoming one spirit with Him. But keeping this union fresh and ever-growing in intimacy takes intentional, quality time daily through prayer, the reading and studying of the Word, and listening to and communion with Him through the Spirit.

But he who is joined to the Lord is one spirit with Him (1 Corinthians 6:17).

When you allow God to marry your spirit with His, you become one in spirit. As a matter of fact, that's why the Bible tells us to walk in the Spirit because you've been united and joined with the Lord. (More on this in Chapter 16 "The Intimacy with God Key.")

This marriage becomes the foundation of your authoritative, dominant, powerful prayer life, and prayer becomes feasting on the Lord and not a struggle.

I encourage you to do two things as you develop a more powerful daily life of prayer. The first is to let your seeking inform and affect your prayer in the asking and knocking realm. Because seeking prayer is the most dynamic and authoritative, it can affect your prayer in the asking and knocking realm. For example, when I received my creative miracle of a new liver, the Holy Spirit informed me what and how to petition for it that evening through seeking prayer. As I started to pray, the Lord said, "Don't ask for healing but ask for a brand-new liver."

In simple faith and words, I said, "Lord, take out this bad liver and replace it with a brand-spanking new one."

Then a creative miracle unfolded instantly. (Read the whole story in Chapter 4 "The Blood of Jesus Christ—The Most Powerful of All Keys.") It was the seeking by my spirit that informed my prayer in the asking realm, and I had miraculous results.

On another occasion, as I sought God, He suddenly stopped me and told me what to do and how to receive my healing from low thyroid or hypothyroidism. In my petitioning prayer, I asked according to what the Lord had told me to do, and I received a creative miracle of a new thyroid gland. The revelation I received through seeking prayer was the key to the breakthrough I achieved in the asking prayer realm. (I've included the whole story in Chapter 19 "Heal the Sick.")

These are just two of the many miraculous results I have experienced in my personal life. The multitudes to which I have ministered have benefited from this prayer dynamic as the Spirit informs my simple prayer with signs and wonders following. This will be the same with you as well if you're intentional in following the wisdom revealed in Ecclesiastes 5:1–3.

The key to seeking prayer is listening and watching for what the Lord is saying or doing.

The second thing I would encourage you to do as you develop a more powerful daily life of prayer is to pray in the Holy Spirit.

> But you, beloved, building yourselves up on your most holy faith, praying in the Holy Spirit, (Jude 1:20).

I can't emphasize enough the importance of praying in the Holy Spirit if you want to be effective not only in hearing God's voice but in prayer. As you continue seeking prayer, cultivating a lifestyle of a union of spirit with the Lord, you'll find that you don't have to ask God for understanding of what you're praying in the Holy Spirit. You're getting an interpretation in your native language.

At that point, you're not only praying in the Spirit, but you're praying with understanding as well. No wonder Paul said he prayed in tongues more than you all. (See 1 Corinthians 14.) I think he had discovered the secret of praying in the Holy Spirit. No wonder he received so much revelation, and by the Spirit, wrote 80 percent of the New Testament.

JESUS IN MY LIVING ROOM

Now let me tell you of the story from the opening of this chapter when Jesus visited me in my living room. Two weeks beforehand, the Lord had told me to get ready to take His revival fire to South Africa. In obedience to God, I packed my suitcase and put it by the door, waiting for God's provision to come so that I could go on His mission.

Then on that hot summer evening in Kampla, Uganda, Africa, the Holy Spirit led me into three days of prayer and fasting. I was preparing for the outpouring of God's power onto my life and ministry that would impact lives and nations. I was in seeking prayer in the living room, utterly yielding to the Holy Spirit to pray with me and through me.

As I sought God by my human spirit, suddenly, there was an open heaven over my house. I was caught in the Spirit, and Jesus stood in front of me. As I looked up, I couldn't see a roof anymore, only beautiful open skies.

The Son of God softly pulled down my chin so that I could look into His eyes. What kindness and blazing love for me as I gazed into them. Oh, what gentleness in His voice as He talked with me about my life and ministry struggles.

I explained to Him how hard life was, telling Him every pain I had ever experienced up to that point in my life. I told Him every need that had not been met even though I had prayed, believed, and even acted on the Word. I poured out to Him every longing and inner-most desire of my heart to love and to serve Him.

I explained how I wasn't fit to do the kind of ministry He wanted me to do, how I had no money, no connections and influence, and that I didn't even know where to start or what to do. I passionately told Him about the poverty, injustice, wars, famine, sicknesses, diseases, and the oppression in the world.

He never interrupted me, judged me, or condemned me. Instead, He listened.

When I had finished, He said, "Andrew, I know, and I understand, and I want you to know that I am with you and will always be with you."

Just before He started ascending into the heavens, He said, "I am sending you to South Africa and the nations, and you will demonstrate My kingdom in power with signs and wonders following.

But when the going gets tough, wait upon Me, wait upon Me, wait upon Me."

We started ascending from the earth into the sky, and I begged Him to take me into heaven with Him. I recounted everything bad in this world that I could think of, hoping He would agree. Being with Him meant more to me than life itself. In His presence, I felt safe, secure, and fully satisfied. I didn't want our interaction to end. Oh, what peace, joy, and love I felt from Him toward me, what glory and power of His presence. I could tell we were entering higher dimensions as the surroundings changed to glorious light, fragrant smells, flowers, and beauty too rich for words to describe.

I told Him I loved Him and just wanted to be with Him forever. Just before we entered the most glorious realm that had so much light and beauty that my eyes could hardly open to see it, He gently and lovingly said, "Andrew, you will come and be with Me forever, but it is not yet your time. Now, go and do what I have commissioned you to do. I will be with you."

He then entered into His glory realm, which I took to be heaven. Suddenly, I found myself on my knees in my living room trembling under the power of God.

Now I understood what John meant when he said he heard a voice calling him to come higher, and suddenly, he was in the spirit in Revelation 4:1–2.

Like in my story above, I was praying in the Spirit and yielded to the Spirit when this sacred encounter with Jesus happened to me through seeking prayer.

Do you desire a deeper reality with God? Seek Him with your spirit. As you do this on a daily basis, you're building your spiritual muscles every time. You'll find that you have gone from praying to God and hoping He hears you to praying with God with power, faith, and authority every time.

As you consistently develop the seeking prayer lifestyle, you'll release God's supernatural power, miracles, victory, healing, and breakthrough as part of your daily life.

Continue with me to the next chapter as I teach you how to unlock the power with the key of obedience.

CHAPTER 13

The Obedience Key

"I WANT YOU TO STAY and do a miracle crusade here," the Holy Spirit instructed me after I had just finished speaking at a three-day conference in Free State, South Africa, and was getting ready to leave town.

I said, "Lord, crusades take months to organize."

"Andrew," He said, "I want you to do a miracle crusade here."

Once He called me by my first name, I knew I better pay attention. So, I responded, "Yes, Lord. What do you want me do?"

"Do what you can. I'll do the rest," He assured me.

I went and shared this assignment with the conference's host pastor and some of the other pastors in the city. Most of them weren't interested in another event, to say the least. The leaders of the big churches with more influence didn't want to participate, I think because they didn't know me and didn't hear me speak at the conference. So, the host pastor, his congregation, and a few laypeople from other churches volunteered to help.

We rented the biggest auditorium we could find in the city, set the date, made flyers, and started sharing the news about the crusade. I was acting in obedience. I even told one of the pastors, "It doesn't matter if it's just five of us. God said we do a crusade, and that's what we're going to do."

We used an auditorium that sat about 6,000 people. The first night, about 500 people showed up. The building looked and felt empty. Among those in attendance were a few who were lame and crippled. However, one woman had a broken neck from a car accident. She was well-known in the city and came from a very prominent and influential family there. They all sat on the front row with her.

Just before I walked from backstage up to the platform to minister, the worship team sang the final worship song, "There's power, power, wonder working power in the blood of the Lamb."

The Holy Spirit said, "A woman in the audience has a broken neck. I want you to go, practice Mark 6:13. Anoint her with oil, and pray for her, and I'll heal her."

Before I share the miracle healing of this woman's broken neck, let me highlight a few thoughts about obedience to you.

THE PRICE IS OBEDIENCE

God identifies faith with obedience. Obedience is the proof of your faith and of your surrender to God. As you surrender to Him, you're going to be faced with a decision because God is going to test your faith and your surrender by giving you practical instructions.

Let us then heed the words of the Holy Spirit through Apostle Paul in Acts 5:32 (NIV): "We are witnesses of these things, and so is the Holy Spirit, whom God has given to those who obey him."

The anointing by the Holy Spirit is given to those who obey God, so the test of your surrender and of your faith is obedience. Then He's going to watch for your action or response. Obedience is the condition of receiving and retaining the anointing upon your life.

When King Saul was disobedient to the Lord, the prophet Samuel said to him, "Has the Lord as great delight in burnt offerings and sacrifices, As in obeying the voice of the Lord? Behold, to obey is better than sacrifice, And to heed than the fat of rams. For rebellion is as the sin of witchcraft, And stubbornness is as iniquity and idolatry. Because you have rejected the word of the Lord, He also has rejected you from being king" (1 Samuel 15:22–23).

Saul lost the throne and the kingdom the moment he disobeyed the word of the Lord. Obedience is the key to receiving and retaining God's power in and through your life as you surrender.

When you have a need or are faced with a situation in your life, start with asking God about it and then listening to His strategy and plan. God may say, "Go do this." If you hesitate, you're going to miss His anointing and blessing for your desired breakthrough, victory, and healing.

Saul was rejected from being king because he wouldn't obey the word of the Lord. God will not anoint those who walk in rebellion or disobedience. Period. He says, "If you have rejected my instructions, I'm going to reject your work."

If you are willing and obedient, You shall eat the good of the land; (Isaiah 1:19).

INQUIRE, LISTEN, AND OBEY IMMEDIATELY.

Obedience is acting out of your faith. You may even want to pause reading this book now and ask the Holy Spirit to help you hear the voice of the Lord.

Dear Holy Spirit, help me and enable me to hear the voice of the Lord and obey immediately.

Like in the story I shared at the beginning of this chapter, what would have happened if I had stuck to my way and preached my message before calling the woman to pray for her? First of all, I would have flat-out disobeyed the practical leading and instructions of the Holy Spirit. Consequently, I know for certain that crusade would have been a miserable failure. Sure, a few people would have gotten saved, healed, and set free, but we would not have had the mighty outpouring of the Holy Spirit and His power that I'll share with you in the next section.

God knew when He told me to do the crusade that I didn't have months to organize it. He knew I didn't have the necessary support of the local leaders that I would normally like to have when holding gospel crusades. He knew I didn't have the right publicity for the event. But He also knew the key to advertising and packing an auditorium to overflow.

All He required and demanded of me was not the greatest organization and publicity but my obedience.

It doesn't matter what you're believing God for. The trigger to releasing God's supernatural power is obedience. Why? Because obedience is your faith in action. Where there is obedience, that is where God is working in power with miracles, signs, and wonders.

MIRACLE HEALING POWER UNLEASHED

Now the rest of the story.

As the music continued to play in the background, I said, "There's a woman here, and you have a broken neck. God wants to heal you right now. Come forward."

The woman sitting on the front row with a huge brace around her neck walked toward me. I did exactly what the Holy Spirit said to do. I got a little oil and anointed her and then laid my hands on her and prayed as the Lord led me for her miracle healing.

When I was done, I told her, "Now, take the brace off."

Her husband standing next to her said, "Well, she has a broken neck."

I said, "Not anymore. Take the brace off."

Her husband helped her to slowly take the brace off her neck.

Then I said, "I want you to do what you couldn't do before."

This woman turned her head back and forth once, twice, and then a third time. During the fourth time, tears of joy rolled down her face. She hadn't been able to turn her head for the past two and half years.

She had gone to several hospitals, saw different specialist, and had sought all kinds of help that money could buy, yet they couldn't fix her. Here we were, and within a few moments, the Holy Ghost perfected this miracle right before the watchful eyes of 500 people. The woman was instantly healed.

Now remember on that first night, we started out with 500 people in the auditorium and had empty seats all over it. The next day, we couldn't fit everyone who came into this auditorium that held over 6,000. There was not enough room. It was so packed, the fire marshal came and said, "You can't put more people in this room."

What was the key? It was obedience to the leading of the Spirit.

The obedience triggered the miracle healing power and manifested the breakthrough that we needed for that specific crusade, but most importantly, for healing of that dear woman. The victory depended on my ability to obey God and to take action.

It doesn't matter where you are or what you're going through right now. If you can get a hold of God's word, what God is saying right now, and obey that word, it releases the miracle-working power of God, which is already in you.

Here, the creative miracle-working power began to flow and touch her neck. She was on cloud nine.

As word about her healing spread, those from the surrounding areas wanted to see what was going on. The crusade that was intended for three days ended up going on every day for three weeks. They had a revival in that city. Prior to that crusade, many leaders told me that they had never seen anything like that in their region.

I can't take any credit. The pastors couldn't take any credit. They didn't even want to get involved and help in the beginning. But as the crusade continued, they started attending one by one as well as their people. We honored them and got them involved in following up with the new converts.

For those three weeks, the city's auditorium became holy ground. God was there! We witnessed hundreds of miracles of healing, deliverance from demon possession and oppression, curses broken off of people, and most importantly, thousands of souls added to the Kingdom of God for the first time.

As for me, God had taken me from an unknown to someone every pastor wanted at their church. Then He said, "Now, you've done your job. Leave town."

The churches reaped a harvest of souls because of that one act of obedience. The glory doesn't cost you a thing, but the anointing does.

The Miracle Worker Holy Spirit is already within you and His power upon you. Unleash it with obedience and action.

What is the last thing that God said about your situation that either needs divine intervention or guidance? What is the last thing God said about your sickness, your disease?

Obey that last word, those practical instructions. Then watch God's power in action on your behalf.

Join me in the next chapter as I show you how to release God's supernatural through the action of faith.

CHAPTER 14

The Activation of Faith Key

"DO WHAT YOU COULDN'T DO before," I say to people after they've been healed, encouraging them to respond after hearing the Word and prayer. As always, I see more miracles when people act out their faith than when they hear the message and get prayer and do nothing.

Here's a case in point. Joseph was visiting Colorado from California, when a friend told him about the upcoming Encounter God's Power meetings. So, he postponed his return back home to attend, hoping for a miracle for the torn ligaments in his left foot that had caused it to point inward. For six months, he hadn't been able to walk properly due the pain. He had been taking pain killers to help numb the pain, and he didn't have insurance for surgery. But a miracle was about to occur.

How did Joseph's miracle healing manifest? More on that in a moment. First, let's explore what faith is, how to get faith that works, and how to unleash it for your desired results.

Receiving and experiencing the anointing is by grace through faith. For any kingdom key to work for you, you need to believe in the God of those principles as well as in the principle itself.

For example, if you don't believe in the blood of Jesus, the blood is not going to do anything for you. If you don't believe in the Word of God, then it won't do anything. If you don't believe in the Holy Spirit, He won't do anything for you.

All kingdom keys, methods, and secrets that I'm sharing in this book all work by grace through faith. God has faith in you, but you need to have faith in your own faith and in the One who has given you those keys for it to work.

WHAT IS FAITH?

Now faith is the assurance (title deed, confirmation) of things hoped for (divinely guaranteed), and the evidence of things not seen [the conviction of their reality—faith comprehends as fact what cannot be experienced by the physical senses] (Hebrews 11:1 AMP).

You might say you believe, but you don't feel anything. That's why it's faith. Faith is not a feeling but the assurance for your desired miracle and the confirmation of your hope.

Sometimes you may feel something, but most of the time you won't. Does it mean that the power of God isn't there? No. Somebody said that faith is the power that moves the hand of God. The power of God is in you, with you, ready to flow through you, but you need to get it in motion by faith.

So, what do you do? I simply glue my spiritual ears onto the Holy Spirit to hear what He is saying. What He is going to instruct me to do?

When I act on the Word, it opens the portals of His power and causes the floodgates to overflow in my life. It's taking place by faith.

But without faith *it is* impossible to please *Him,* for he who comes to God must believe that He is, and *that* He is a rewarder of those who diligently seek Him (Hebrews 11:6).

HOW TO GET FAITH FOR THE IMPOSSIBLE

The key lies in this simple truth—hearing and hearing by the Word of God.

So then faith *comes* by hearing, and hearing by the word of God (Romans 10:17).

We all desire to have faith that moves mountains. We all want to walk in the power of God with miraculous results. But how are we to get and maintain such faith?

I believe this hearing is not only for the preached word but also the (rhema) word with which the Spirit speaks. It could be through the written word He speaks at that moment which, in turn, becomes rhema to you. It could be a prophetic word or a word of knowledge that comes directly to you or someone else. However you get a word, it comes with power and faith when you receive it, believe it, and act upon it.

To have victorious, ever-increasing faith, the previous verse (Romans 10:17) tells us that faith comes by hearing and hearing by the Word of God. God wants us to learn to hear so that we can hear and keep on hearing His Word. We thereby are given the supernatural impartation of God's own faith to receive and manifest His kingdom realities on Earth as it is in heaven daily. So, hear His voice and walk in power and faith daily.

UNLEASH GOD'S POWER
BY ACTING OUT YOUR FAITH

Let's go back to Joseph's miracle story from the beginning of this chapter and see how he was instantly healed by his own faith. To begin, Joseph listened intently as I preached the message "Jesus Is Our Healer—Jehovah Rapha."

Afterward, I gave a call for salvation. Then I instructed everyone in the audience who needed healing or a touch from God to place one hand where the pain, sickness, or disease was and raise the other hand to the Lord.

I said, "Get ready to experience the healing power and life of Jesus the Healer."

I didn't lay hands on anyone but prayed a general prayer for healing, deliverance, and freedom from oppressions. Once I had finished praying, I asked those who needed a divine touch of God to start doing what they could only do before their affliction.

Joseph started walking back and forth in the back of the auditorium a few times. Then he started running back and forth, faster and faster and faster. I invited him to come and tell us what was happening to him. He said he believed the message I preached, and he was acting out his faith. I was amazed when he told me that when I prayed and released the power of God, he felt fire in his foot. It wasn't completely healed until he got up and started walking on it without using his walking stick.

He testified that the more he walked back and forth, the more the fire in his foot intensified until he couldn't help but start running. At the time of giving his testimony, his foot was completely healed and restored back into its proper position. It was no longer pointing inward. The ligaments were completely restored.

Like Joseph, you too can release God's supernatural by acting out your faith. You don't pray for faith. There is nowhere in the Bible where God says to pray for faith, but He does tell us in Romans 10:17 that faith comes by hearing and hearing by the Word of God.

Do you want to have victorious, ever-increasing, dominant, and creative faith? Hear the Word of God.

Remember that to believe is to act out your faith. The word "believe" is a verb, which means "to do"; it's an action word. If you believe, you act. But it's not enough to believe in the Word; you must have faith in your own faith and that it is enough.

Most of the time, we have faith in everyone else's faith except our own. It's easier to believe that if the pastor will pray for me, or if I can get enough people praying with me and for me, I'll receive the breakthrough I need. Yes, it's biblical to seek prayer support from other believers, but my encouragement for you is not to only rely on other people's faith but also your own. Let me encourage you that your faith is as good as everyone else's. You just need to believe that God honors your faith the same way He'll honor the strongest faith of any person you know. Your faith is enough.

As a matter of fact, with all the miracles Jesus performed for people, it wasn't His faith that healed them or set them free; it was the receiver's own faith. (See Matthew 9:22, 29; Mark 5:34, 10:52; and Luke 7:50, 8:25, 48, 17:19, 18:42.)

There's an action tied to your faith. If you believe the promises of God, then you act on the Word. I urge you to activate and release the anointing through action. If you desire to heal the sick, then go find somebody sick in their body, lay hands on them, and release the miracle power of the healing Jesus that is already in you. If you desire healing in your own body, then use the keys and steps in these chapters that show you how to minister healing to yourself. These are biblical methods of unleashing miracles as you allow the Spirit to lead you to His way of healing and setting you free. Then release your faith and act in obedience, and watch what God will do for you.

Now join me in the next chapter as we explore another fundamental kingdom key to releasing heaven on Earth—the act of binding and loosing.

CHAPTER 15

The Binding and Loosing Key

"MY NAME IS JOY. I'm a sixty-seven-year-old woman who has suffered depression for as long as I can remember. I was diagnosed officially with bipolar depression fifteen years ago but have been in counseling and therapy and treated for regular depression since my late teens. When you put your hand on my shoulder, when you prayed for me, I felt an amazing jolt, then a sense of peace and happiness," Joy testified.

What happened to Joy was truly miraculous. I'll get more into her whole story in a little while and how heaven's reality touched her life and healed her. First, I'd like to discuss how to release heaven on Earth.

"I will give you the keys of heaven's kingdom realm to forbid on earth that which is forbidden in heaven, and to release on earth that which is released in heaven" (Matthew 16:19 TPT).

The New King James Bible (NKJV) renders it this way: "And I will give you the keys of the Kingdom of heaven, and whatever you bind on earth will be bound in heaven, and whatever you loose on earth will be loosed in heaven."

"Does this include me?" I asked my pastor when I was a young believer and starting to minister to my fellow students.

"Yes," he replied. "It includes you and everyone who believes in Jesus Christ."

This was a game changer. For weeks, I thought this promise was too good to be true, but it was true.

So if I've been given the keys to heaven's kingdom realm, to forbid on Earth that which is forbidden in heaven and to release on Earth that which is released in heaven, then I could change my life and my world.

I went to work. I began to search out in Scripture what is in the Kingdom of heaven and what is not.

JESUS PREACHED THE KINGDOM OF HEAVEN

From that time on, Jesus began to proclaim His message with these words: "Keep turning away from your sins and come back to God, for heaven's kingdom realm is now accessible" (Matthew 4:17 TPT).

HEAVEN'S KINGDOM REALM IS ACCESSIBLE

If heaven's realm and all its realities are readily accessible, then our part is to use the keys that have been given to us to "forbid and release" or "bind and loose." Let us heed this commission of Jesus.

"And as you go, preach this message: 'Heaven's kingdom realm is accessible, close enough to touch.' You must continually bring healing to lepers and to those who are sick, and make it your habit to break off the demonic presence from people, and raise the dead back to life. Freely you have received the power of the kingdom, so freely release it to others" (Matthew 10:7–8 TPT).

When I discovered this one component of God's power—binding and loosing, or forbidding and releasing—everything changed for me. The demonstration of that anointing exploded in my life, in my daily interactions, and in my ministry to others.

The keys to unlock heaven's realm in all things, for all things, and regarding all things are in your hands. Remember the Lord's prayer model Jesus gave us? It doesn't involve spending time fighting demons. He shows that when we pray, we are to bring down heaven's kingdom (realm or realities) on Earth and His will to be done on Earth as it is in heaven. (See Matthew 6: 9–13.)

This is how we do spiritual warfare. We focus on the King and His realm and bring His realities on earth. Spiritual warfare is simply enforcing heaven's kingdom realm here on Earth as it is in heaven.

We can't be consumed with pulling down strongholds and fighting demons. Otherwise, we'll have stagnant lives and ministries because we took our eyes off the victory that Jesus has already won.

The devil knows he's defeated though he'll try to put up a fight. However, with the correct knowledge and kingdom keys and belief in the gospel and Christ's finished work, we can wage war on the enemy. We step out in power, faith, and authority to enforce that victory.

"BE THE ANSWER TO YOUR PRAYERS," HE SAID.

Every Friday for seven years, I led all-night prayer meetings in our church with other ministers until a nationwide revival broke out in Uganda.

One evening after praying for the salvation of our community, calling forth people to get saved, and binding the demonic spirits that were oppressing them, I heard the Lord say, "Now, go be the answer to your prayers. You are asking me to do what I have already done. This is now your part, which I commissioned you to do. I will be with you to confirm the Word with miracles, signs and wonders."

We thought we were doing spiritual warfare in our prayer meetings, but the real warfare was when we got out in the streets and into the hospitals, prisons, marketplaces, and open-air crusades with the good news. We were face to face with principalities, powers, and spiritual wickedness in high places. We went where the people were facing impossible situations, and we used the keys of heaven in our hands to release its realities.

Then lo and behold, we began to see strongholds come down, mighty harvests of souls, healings, deliverance, and community revival and transformation. But we had to act. We had to mix our all-night prayers with action in communities where the enemy was holding people captive.

The keys to unlock heaven's kingdom realm are in the hands of every believer to use to usher in heaven's realities in their own lives and for others. Sadly, not many Bible-believing Christians know how to use or engage this biblical power key. My goal in this chapter is to challenge and encourage you to be intentional with it for releasing heaven on Earth.

So how do we use this key of binding and loosing?

RELEASE HEAVEN ON EARTH WITH YOUR WORDS AND ACTIONS

We speak with authority and faith to bind and loose or forbid and release. It's that simple. You have the authority and power in you through the indwelling Christ.

The Holy Spirit moves when you speak. His power is carried and transmitted in your words. Because you have the key to heaven's reality, now you can speak to the spirit of infirmity to come out of your body or someone else's body and then release the healing, freedom, and peace in the place of that infirmity.

JOY'S HEALING STORY

Now let us continue with Joy's story. She said, "My mother and I suffer from severe migraine headaches. In addition, my maternal grandfather raped me from the age of three until nine when my mother found out. He had done the same thing to her. These incestual rapes and her severe migraine headaches led her to commit suicide.

"On the morning of my mother's suicide, she had asked me to come home and watch my three younger siblings while she took a bath. They were four, two and a half, and eleven months old. Being nine years old, I didn't question.

"They were very loud and hard to control. I went upstairs to get my mother, but the bathroom door was locked. I was panicking, so my dad came home early only to discover that she had committed suicide with his shotgun.

"I blamed myself well into my adulthood. Fortunately, I had a wonderful father, and a couple of years later, a terrific stepmother. All of this hurt and pain was the reason my life was entrenched in deep depression and migraine headaches for years."

Joy listened to me as I taught the message called "Christ in Us." I showed the audience what Christ in us means for them and how to access Christ's indwelling life and power that's already in their lives.

After the message, I ministered to the sick in prayer by releasing that same healing life and power of Christ. It would permeate their souls and entire bodies until they were completely and perfectly healed.

Joy continued. "At the end of the Sunday service on October 27, 2019, you asked if anyone wanted healing. I did and came forward. Since that time, and it's been over a month now, I have not taken any antidepressants, mood stabilizers, or calm downers of any kind. I am completely healed. I am happy with Jesus and migraine free as well! Thank you, Jesus and Andrew!"

EXERCISE FOR BINDING AND LOOSING HEAVEN'S REALITIES

If you're new to the idea of speaking what heaven says, then binding and loosing heaven's realities might be hard for you to do in the beginning. But with daily and intentional practice of this principle, it will become part of your daily life over time as you live out God's Kingdom where you work, live, and play. It doesn't matter who you are or where you are spiritually. You can release heaven on Earth with your mouth, words, faith, and actions, but you have to speak. Until then, the Holy Spirit doesn't have anything to work with.

You have partnered with heaven. The Spirit of God goes to work by releasing Christ's life and His power to work on your behalf.

Join me in the next chapter as I show you how your intimacy with God gives you another key to catching and releasing His supernatural.

CHAPTER 16

The Intimacy with God Key

"MARRY ME, SON. Marry me."

"Yes, Lord, I will marry you," I responded.

It was a cool spring morning in 2003, and I was finishing my morning prayer. As I was getting off my knees, the Lord kept repeating His invitation to marry Him.

I answered with what I thought was the right response. In my mind, I thought about when a man proposes to a woman for marriage. He asks, "Will you marry me?" Most times, she says, "Yes. I'll marry you."

But I heard the Holy Spirit repeatedly say, "Andrew, marry me." This went on for about five years. I heard the invitation more times than I can count during that time, and I began to get frustrated with myself.

One evening, I said, "Okay, God. You've asked me to marry you, and I said I would, but you continue to ask. What am I missing?"

He said, "I just want you to marry me."

Then I realized that all this time, I had been giving the wrong answer. My answer was for the future—I *will* marry you (future tense)—and He wanted me to marry Him now.

Once I understood, I said, "God, show me what it means to marry You in the Scripture."

Instantly, I heard in my spirit, "Open the Bible, and read Hosea 2:14–20."

When I did, lo and behold, the invitation was scriptural. I then reread the whole chapter to get the full context. I told God, "Yes, Lord, I marry you right now."

For five long years, the Lord had been so patient, persistent, and loving to keep asking me. During this time, I had been seeking complete healing from the many injuries I had suffered from as a result of a car accident. (I shared this story with you in Chapter 5 "The Holy Spirit Key" and Chapter 6 "The Worship and Holy Communion Key.") I was in what felt like a desert experience without an end in sight. In this wilderness, God was with me.

In Hosea 2:14, God says, "Therefore, behold, I will allure her, Will bring her into the wilderness, And speak comfort to her." The NIV renders it this way ". . . I will lead her into the wilderness and speak tenderly to her." Here I was in my wilderness, and He was pursuing me and tenderly speaking comfort to me.

You too can know God's hope, love, restoration, and healing in the midst of your battles, adversity, and trials. The secret is marrying God. Allow Him to intensify your relationship with Him so that you are one with Him. In this place of intimacy, this is what's going to happen according to Hosea 2:15: "Then I will give her back her vineyards from there, And the Valley of Achor (pain, trouble) a door of hope and expectation. She shall sing there and respond as in the days of her youth, As in the day when she came up from the land of Egypt" (emphasis mine).

The first thing that happens is that He gives you your vineyards, which represents your heart. Your broken and wounded heart is restored as He puts you back together. Then your pain is healed. Your troubles become a door of hope into your future. You begin to sing a new song of love. In Hosea 2:16, you're married to Him, and He becomes your husband: "And it shall be, in that day," Says the Lord, "*That you will call Me 'My Husband,' And no longer call Me 'My Master.'*"

In this intimate desert place, you're captivated by His heart of love. You know you're loved, known, belong not as a stranger or even a servant in His house but as a lovely bride who has been purchased by the most precious bride price of all—the blood of Jesus. You'll know His divine protection, and your heart will respond in love to the One who betrothed you in righteousness, justice, loving-kindness, and faithfulness forever. As a result of this divine intimate exchange, you shall know the Lord (Hosea 2:17–20).

The most important thing of all that you can do for yourself is to grow in intimacy with the Lord daily. This begins with a yes in your heart to marry Him now, not in the future. He wants to captivate you with His heart, His passion, thoughts, feelings, and emotions for you and for others. He desires to speak tenderly to you and comfort you. He wants to restore those broken places in your life, but He demands your responsive heart to Him.

How can you grow in intimacy with God daily in addition to the obvious practice of prayer and reading and studying His Word? Here's one key that I think will help you in your daily intimate pursuit of God:

BE OF ONE SPIRIT WITH THE LORD

Because your most intimate connection with the Lord takes place in the depth of your spirit, keeping a constant union with His Spirit is paramount.

> But one who joins himself to the Lord is one spirit with Him (1 Corinthians 6: 17 NASB).

When you allow God to marry your spirit with His, you become one in spirit. In this place of union, walking in His power, hearing His voice, and walking in the Spirit becomes part of your daily life.

[Hush!] Be silent before the Lord GOD [there is no acceptable excuse to offer] . . . (Zephaniah 1:7 AMP).

But the LORD is in His holy temple. Let all the earth hush *and* be silent before Him (Habakkuk 2:20 AMP).

Now your spirit is overflowing with the Spirit of God because of the union. You know the reality of His glory, power, wisdom, faith, and authority. So how do you get to be united with the Lord in spirit?

INVITE THE HOLY SPIRIT TO UNITE YOU WITH THE LORD IN SPIRIT ON A DAILY BASIS.

Dear Holy Spirit, unite my spirit with Yours according to the Word of God, that I may be one spirit with You, the Lord Jesus and Father God now and for all eternity.

As a believer in Christ, you need to receive that uniting daily by faith. You do this by communing and yielding to the Holy Spirit to continually keep you joined with the Lord in spirit. This is how you stay on fire for the Lord. The Holy Spirit sustains your unity of spirit with the Lord.

When you unite with the Lord every day, you'll discover and experience a new relationship and friendship with God and the Holy Spirit. I didn't know this until the Holy Spirit revealed this truth to me. After He did, it was the opening of the floodgates of God's heart to me.

I encourage you to be in a quiet place and relaxed and to yield to the Holy Spirit during this time. This isn't so much about praying as we know prayer. This is communion and receiving by faith. This is part of your inheritance. You are united with the Lord in spirit, so let Him captivate you and speak tenderly to you.

At the beginning of this chapter, God pursued me to bring me into a deeper place of intimacy and union of spirit with Him. All it took was a responsive heart with a yes. When I responded to God's invitation, He released strategies through which He would manifest my healing as I followed His practical instructions. Restoration began in my life on every level.

I believe God is calling you to a deeper place of intimacy that will further empower and elevate your life to catch and release God's supernatural power daily and become your best in Christ. As you continue to read this book, I believe God is extending a fresh invitation to you, saying, "Marry me."

Let us continue to the next chapter where I discuss absolute surrender and how it's another key to walking in God's supernatural.

CHAPTER 17
The Absolute Surrender Key

"PREPARE THE VESSEL, and I will do the ministry," I heard the still small voice whisper to my spirit.

Initially, I didn't understand what was meant by "prepare my vessel." Naturally, I asked, "Lord, what do you mean to prepare the vessel? How do I prepare the vessel?"

He answered by pointing me to the Word in Romans 6:13 and Luke 22:42. More on these Scriptures in a moment.

I first saw this kingdom power key in action when I went to minister to a church of several hundred people in Uganda. Everyone, including the senior pastor who was interpreting for me on the pulpit, got touched by the Holy Spirit and fell down under the mighty power of God.

What did I do for such a move of God to happen? I surrendered. From the moment I stepped onto the pulpit, I kept repeating, "I love you, Jesus. I love you, Jesus. I love you, Jesus." And that was it! Read the whole story in my book *Working the Works of God* where I get into more details in Chapter 7, "Understanding God's Grace," on pages 54–58.

In that Uganda church service, the sick were healed, the demonically oppressed and captives were set free, souls were saved, and I didn't even preach a message.

I have come to learn over the years that if there's any other key that's going to give you God's power, it's absolute surrender and dying to self daily. If we're going to know God's power day in and day out, we need to live a surrendered life. True surrender doesn't involve giving up one thing to God. It's turning over to God all of your inward self. That includes your heart, your mind, your intellect, your will, your emotions, your conscious, even your subconscious as well as your whole body.

> ...but yield yourselves unto God, as those that are alive from the dead, and your members as instruments of righteousness unto God (Romans 6:13).

So, the great secret of blessedness and power is found in this verse, in these words, "yield yourselves unto God." In the English Standard Version (ESV), the word "yield" is rendered "present."

The Amplified Bible (AMP) renders it as "offer." You offer yourself to God. This is a willing act on your part. You volunteer yourself. You willingly turn yourself over to God. He's not coercing you. That's why it's absolute surrender because you're surrendering your consent. What does that mean? It means you're putting yourself at God's disposal.

You might be full of the Holy Spirit. You might practice the blood, the Word of God, but if you can't surrender to God, you're going to miss out on the full function of the anointing's overflow. Surrender yourself entirely to God, to be His property, for Him to fill you with His Spirit and power, and to use you as He wills.

This is paramount, but how do you fully surrender to God? You lose your life so that you can find it in Christ in God.

> "All who seek to live apart from me will lose it all. But those who let go of their lives for my sake and surrender it all to me will discover true life!" (Matthew 10:39 TPT).

A friend of mine said to me, "I can't surrender to God because it's like when I do, all hell's going to break loose."

That's not true, but to the flesh, it will feel like all hell is breaking loose because you're putting yourself at God's disposal. The flesh doesn't want what the Spirit wants. When you surrender, God begins to empty your house, right? He's going to begin to take out everything in you and around you that hinders that love, that hinders His power, that's contrary to His name, His nature, His life, and to Himself so that He can fill you with Himself and use you.

So He has to empty you of everything else before He can fill you and anoint you. Otherwise, He'll be putting new wine into old wine skin. The wine will ferment, and the old wine skin will burst. God will lose both the vessel and the wine.

God loves you too much to let that happen. But when you approach God in surrender, you are losing your life, so to speak. When you put your life at God's disposal, you're going to feel like you've lost it. That's why I believe Jesus used those words "lose your life" in Matthew 10:39. You're going to feel like you're not in control of it. You're turning it over to Christ.

We as seekers in His promise have great hope. "If you try to save your life, you will lose it. But if you give it up for me, you will surely find it" (Matthew 10:39 CEV).

Find it where? Find it in Christ. That's why Colossians 3:3 says that our lives are hidden in Christ, in God, for those who surrender it.

HOW DO YOU COMPLETELY SURRENDER YOUR LIFE TO GOD?

We can learn from our precious master Jesus Christ. He couldn't carry out His earthly ministry as the Lamb of God who took away the sins of the world until He surrendered. Likewise, you and I can't fulfill the Great Commission and continue living the Christ life and fulfill His ministry on Earth without absolute surrender to Him.

So how did Jesus die to self or surrender? Let us look no further than God's Word:

> "Father, if you will, please don't make me suffer by having me drink from this cup. But do what you want, and not what I want" (Luke 22:42 CEV).

> ". . . Father, if it is Your will, take this cup away from Me; nevertheless not My will, but Yours, be done" (Luke 22:42).

ABSOLUTE SURRENDER IS LOSING YOUR WILL TO THE WILL OF GOD.

When Jesus said, "Nevertheless not My will, but Yours be done," He was a dead man. The flesh was dead. It was no longer His will. It was no longer His way, His desires. It was God's will from that moment on. He lost His will to the will of His Father in heaven.

After that death to self, there was no pain or agony He would face that He had not already experienced in His death to self.

If you're still giving conditions to God, that's not surrender. Absolute surrender isn't about surrendering one thing but about surrendering everything. That's why the Bible says in Romans 6:13 to "present yourself."

You might say, "But I surrendered my mind. I surrendered my money. I surrendered my marriage. I surrendered my ministry, my call."

That's great, but that's not absolute surrender. He wants everything so that He can have your will in everything, for everything, and regarding everything lost to Him.

DIE DAILY.

Apostle Paul died daily. We can too.

> I assure you, believers, by the pride which I have in you in [your union with] Christ Jesus our Lord, I die daily [I face death and die to self] (1 Corinthians 15:31 AMP).

Do you want to experience the anointing in an all new way like you've never known? Do you long to release God's supernatural power daily? Use this kingdom key. Die to self every day. How do you do this?

SURRENDER TO GOD AND DIE TO SELF DAILY.

Will you yield now? Here's a prayer you can use:

> *Heavenly Father, from now on, I have no will of my own. Your will be done in me, through me, by me, and regarding me in all things. I put myself unreservedly in Your hands. Now anoint me afresh with the power of the Holy Spirit according to Your Word, through the blood of Jesus Christ, Your Son. In Jesus's name, amen.*

Now that we've learned more about the power of Jesus and the keys He has given us, continue with me to the next section in this book. I'll put all of these keys together so that we can unleash the miracle worker in us, heal the sick (including ourselves), cast out demons and set the captives free, and release God's signs, miracles, and wonders every single day.

SECTION III
THE ACCESS

CHAPTER 18

Unleash the Miracle Worker within You

"THE POWER OF GOD is right where you are," I declared boldly by faith while preaching at a crusade in Nairobi, Kenya. With those simple words, the unlimited of power of the Miracle Worker—the Holy Spirit—was unleashed. Many people in the crowd started falling under the power of God. It was so mighty that as a satanist made his way to the pulpit to kill me, it lifted him from the front of the auditorium and carried him all the way to the back. In fact, God "kicked" him out of there without hurting him in any way. The scene reminded me of those science fiction superhero movies when the bad guy was sent flying in the air by the good guy and landed on his back. That's what happened to this satanist. Many people knew him, so nobody dared touch him.

Before I share what happened next, let me walk you through another kingdom principle to unleash the miracle worker within you.

You too can walk in the believer's power all the way into the double portion of the kingly anointing of Jesus. Remember, the kingly anointing is the greatest. But then you can have a double portion of that.

What exactly does "double portion" mean? Basically, it's the amount of activity and intensity of power that the anointing is going to manifest in and through your life.

Remember, Jesus said in John 14:12 that we would do greater works than Him. Those of you who are pressing into God to receive the double portion, you'll do the greater works. You'll function with the operation of the Spirit in your life, and it's going to produce double activity, double results of what He did.

I believe that's what He wants for all of us. Whatever God has called you to do, whether a homemaker, school teacher, carpenter, businessman, doctor, or civil servant, a double portion to God's power is waiting for you to be effective and fruitful with maximum impact for His glory.

I'm telling you, you can have it. Do you need to experience Holy Spirit power today? Connect with the source.

> But when the Holy Spirit has come upon you, you will receive power to testify about me with great effect, to the people in Jerusalem, throughout Judea, in Samaria, and to the ends of the earth, about my death and resurrection (Acts 1:8 TLB).

I believe that the Holy Spirit and His power are the final and last gift to the Church before Jesus comes. I also believe that the Holy Spirit is the greatest gift to us as believers since Christ. His power and work are so paramount that Jesus said, "I'm leaving, but I'm not going to leave you as orphans." (See John 14:18–19 and John 15:25–27.)

Why? Because you're going to need the Holy Spirit and what He'll do in you, with you, for you, and through you to be able to become your best, to do and to receive all that He had paid for.

From beginning to the end, succeeding is not by might nor by power but by the power of the Spirit.

Then he said, "This is God's message to Zerubbabel: 'Not by might, nor by power, but by my Spirit, says the Lord Almighty—you will succeed because of my Spirit, though you are few and weak'" (Zechariah 4:6 TLB).

Success is by the Spirit as He empowers, leads, and guides you in every aspect of your life. It's paramount for us to know the Holy Spirit, to have a relationship with Him, to be baptized in the Holy Spirit, to walk in unity with the Holy Spirit, and to be able to hear the voice of the Holy Spirit.

Success is not by your cleverness. It's not by strength of the human arm. It's by the Holy Spirit. The Lord told Zerubbabel that though they were few and weak, he would succeed. The Holy Spirit is going to empower you in the same way He did Zerubbabel. He's going to help you and enable you to be successful in your Christian life and service.

HOW TO EXPERIENCE THE POWER OF THE SPIRIT DAILY

Remember that the Holy Spirit is the source of power in your life. So how do we experience this power every day?

Let me share with you several ways that are not covered elsewhere in the book. They have served me well for over thirty-three years, and I believe they'll also help you to cultivate a lifestyle of power. Then I'll show you the simple methods of unleashing that power.

1. SURRENDER TO THE HOLY SPIRIT EVERY DAY.

Many believers want to access the power of the Spirit without turning themselves over to Him. Yet He desires to clothe Himself with you like He did with Gideon.

"Surrender" or "yield" means for you to put yourself at His disposal. He can bring you into Himself. See what the Spirit did with Gideon in Judges 6:34 (AMP): "So the Spirit of the LORD clothed

Himself with Gideon [and empowered him]; and he blew a trumpet, and the Abiezrites were called together [as a militia] to follow him."

Did you notice that it wasn't Gideon clothing himself with the Holy Spirit? It was the Holy Spirit clothing Himself with Gideon. In other words, the Holy Spirit took Gideon as His property, His home, and Gideon became His body.

That's why we're the temple of the Holy Spirit (1 Corinthians 6:19). The Holy Spirit clothes Himself with us, and we are clothed in Him. By the Spirit, Paul urged other believers to walk in the Spirit. (See Galatians 5:16, 25.)

How are you supposed to walk in the Spirit when He's outside of you? It's impossible. The only way we can walk in the Spirit is if and when we yield completely to Him so that He can clothe Himself with us. He becomes the center of our being, and as a result, we're clothed with His life and power as Jesus promised in Luke 24:49 (NIV): "I am going to send you what my Father has promised; but stay in the city until you have been clothed with power from on high."

The angel told Gideon he was going to go help deliver God's people. Gideon gave an excuse and said, "I'm the least in my family. I come from the smallest clan— Manasseh. I can't be used by God." His response wasn't much different from others I've encountered.

They say to me: "I can't be anointed because I don't have this or that."

You know, the anointing is not a monopoly for a few. You can be anointed, and I'm showing you how. This is key; put it in your spirit. Every believer who desires the anointing can be anointed to the highest level.

This weak man Gideon, who thought he couldn't be the commander in chief, the Holy Spirit clothed Himself with him, and then he became a force to be reckoned with.

You walk in the Spirit because the Spirit clothes Himself with you. That's why Jesus told the disciples to wait for the Holy Spirit to come upon them because when He comes, He's going to clothe them (Luke 24:49).

Clothe the disciples with what? Clothe them with Himself, and as a result, they were clothed with His power. The Holy Spirit was and still is the applicator of the power of God.

So, in communion with the Holy Spirit, you may want to pray something like this:

Dear Holy Spirit, I surrender myself completely to You—spirit, soul, and body. I yield my natural and spiritual senses to You. Clothe me with Your glory, and fill me afresh with the power of Your presence.

2. ACKNOWLEDGE THE PRESENCE OF THE HOLY SPIRIT.

Next, practice His presence. How do you do that?

The Holy Spirit is a person, not an "it," not an energy or a mist, but a person with all the faculties that make up a person, such as heart, mind, will, emotions, feelings, and intellect. So, respond to Him in the same way you would to a real person.

Embrace and receive the Holy Spirit as a person, not as wind, breath, and oil (though those are part of His manifestations). When you connect with Him on that level, you unlock the fullness of His life.

So how do you acknowledge His presence? The same way we practice the presence of God the Father and Jesus—by recognizing and acknowledging His person and presence in you, with you, and upon you. I can recognize and acknowledge His presence by saying, "Holy Spirit, I thank you for being with me right now." (More on this in the next point.)

"the Spirit of truth, whom the world cannot receive, because
it neither sees Him nor knows Him; but you know Him, for
He dwells with you and will be in you" (John 14:17).

When you acknowledge His presence, you stop ignoring and ne-
glecting Him. Begin acknowledging Him in you, with you, and His
power upon you. Let Him know that you know He's not out there;
He's closer than any part of your members. With this recognition, you
begin to engage His life and resources. A door then opens to a divine
exchange that you have never dreamt about or experienced.

One of the basic needs that humans have is to be validated, to
be known and to belong. Since the Holy Spirit is not a human but
a person, He too longs for and desires your recognition. He wants to
know that you validate His presence. He loves when you tell Him how
much you value Him and cherish His life, presence, power, and work in
you and with you. He's delighted when you tell Him how valuable He
is to you, when you acknowledge and recognize Him.

You see, if you ignore someone and don't value them, they're going to be less and less effective in your life. They're going to feel less
important, less needed, and their productivity and level of engagement
are going to go down. But if you validate them with words of affirma-
tion and acts of appreciation, saying, "I really appreciate your work. I
appreciate your efforts," what happens? Your validation makes them
feel good, so they want to be involved more. They want to work more
because you appreciate their efforts, and you value them and what they
do. You recognize and acknowledge their involvement.

The Holy Spirit doesn't live for validation, but your acknowledge-
ment and recognition release Him to be who He wants to be for you,
who He wants to be in you, and who He wants to be with you and
through you. It's simple but powerful.

So acknowledge, recognize, and appreciate the Holy Spirit as you go through the day, and you'll know exponentially the power of the Spirit in you, with you, and upon you.

3. ADMIT THE HOLY SPIRIT INTO FELLOWSHIP WITH YOU.

May the grace of the Lord Jesus Christ, and the love of God, and the fellowship of the Holy Spirit be with you all (2 Corinthians 13:14 NIV).

We talk a lot about fellowship with the Holy Spirit, but nowhere in the Bible does it say we have fellowship with the Holy Spirit. We have fellowship with Jesus and the Father (1 John 1:3, 6 and 1 John 2:24), but the Bible says that the fellowship of the Holy Spirit is with us.

Now, this is key to experiencing the power daily. You have the fellowship of the Holy Spirit with you. So how do you get this fellowship? You fellowship with the Holy Spirit as you admit Him into fellowship with you. You allow Him to fellowship with you, and then you begin to fellowship back with Him.

Your greatest need is the fullness of the fire and power of the Holy Spirit in your life. But how can you or any believer obtain this divine power of God? It all starts with the baptism of the Holy Spirit and then continues through the communion in the Holy Spirit with you. The result is His fire and unlimited power in and upon your life.

As you fellowship in return, He then brings you into His position, His environment. He brings you into His world, so to speak.

"Fellowship" means communion, comradeship, and partnership. The Holy Spirit comes into communion with you. He's your comrade, friend, and partner in life, in marriage, business, ministry, and everything else concerning you. As a comrade, He shares in your battles. As a friend, He shares in your trials. As a partner, He shares in your work.

In partnerships, the members share the resources of the other, so it is with the partnership of the Spirit with you. The moment you welcome His partnership, you begin to share His resources in a greater measure, whether it be power, wisdom, guidance, faith, and this list is long. As you put yourself at His disposal, He puts Himself at your disposal. You experience the law of reciprocity.

You express your deep longing, concern, cares, and struggles and listen for His wisdom, guidance, and strategy. Likewise, He'll share with you His heart and mind, what makes Him sad, what grieves, quenches, or offends Him, and also what He loves about you, your family, your business, and your ministry. There is a reciprocal response from your heart to His and from His heart back to yours. This is the most intimate level you can experience with God through the Holy Spirit. (More on that in Chapter 16 "The Intimacy with God Key.")

I remember when God unlocked this truth to me. My response was as simple as saying, "Holy, Spirit, I yield myself to You. Commune with me as You will. I welcome Your friendship. I welcome Your communion. I welcome You to teach me."

This is not prayer, which we know as petitioning. This is fellowship. You admit Him into fellowship. He's not going to push Himself on you.

Many people are trying to walk in the anointing without knowing the Holy Spirit. But this is key—the fellowship of the Holy Spirit is with you. Welcome His communion, welcome His teaching, His help. Just welcome Him to partner with you. That's why the Bible says in Mark 16:20 that the Lord worked with them. They didn't work with the Lord. Why? Because the Holy Spirit had fellowship with them.

The Holy Spirit worked with them. As a result, miracles, signs, and wonders were manifesting. The same applies to you and me.

Welcome the Holy Spirit into your world, into your life, into your space daily.

Talk to Him: "Holy Spirit, what are you thinking? What are you feeling?" Right there He gets to talk to you about what He feels, what He thinks, what He desires, and what His plans are for you or someone else you are praying for.

This is the lifestyle I desire for you to cultivate if you haven't already started so that you can release God's supernatural through the anointing all the time.

4. PURSUE INTIMACY WITH HOLY SPIRIT.

The Holy Spirit brings you to where He fellowships with your spirit in an intimate way. This level is where real intimacy with God is cultivated. It begins with acknowledging the Holy Spirit and then allowing Him to fellowship with you.

I encourage you to pursue that intimacy with the Spirit in the same way you pursue it with Jesus, in the same way you pursue it with the Father. Pursue it with the Holy Spirit.

The Bible says, "But the one who joins himself to the Lord is one spirit *with Him*" (1 Corinthians 6:17 NASB). Also, the Bible says, "Now the Lord is the Spirit, and where the Spirit of the Lord *is*, there *is* liberty" (2 Corinthians 3:17 NASB).

The Spirit is in you. When you seek intimacy with Him, you allow Him to invade your space, your time, and your world. Then He can bring you into His world of revelation, power, love, His fruit, and His acts and works. He's going to anoint and intimately rub or smear His power in you and upon you. That's why Jesus told His disciples, "… But stay in the city until you are clothed with power from on high" (Luke 24:49).

In this clothing, a marriage takes place, a divine entwining of personalities. He takes possession of you like He did with Gideon. Then Gideon went from a weakling to the commander in chief to defeating the armies of God's enemies (Judges 6:34). Why? Because the Holy Spirit clothed Himself with Gideon.

YIELD AND RECEIVE THE POWER OF THE HOLY SPIRIT THROUGH COMMUNION.

Be intentional in yielding and receiving the power of the Holy Spirit by faith in communion with the Spirit. The power of God is not a monopoly of a chosen few in the body of Christ. It's for all those who desire to have it. Jesus died and opened the portals of heaven so that all of us can have access to the throne room and receive God's power. While doing communion and speaking to the Holy Spirit, say,

Dear Holy Spirit, I put myself at Your absolute disposal. Empty me of all inward self or selfishness that hinders Your love, Your passion, Your person, Your presence, and Your power in my life. Wonderful Lord, clothe Yourself with me now and take possession of me. Fill me with Your power so that I may witness for Christ effectively from this moment on. Amen.

HOW TO UNLEASH THE MIRACLE WORKER IN YOU

My story at the beginning of this chapter is one of so many experiences in my personal life and in my ministry around the world. I shared it to show you that it is so simple to unleash the power of God that is already in you.

There is no right or wrong way of doing it. You do two things to unlock the miracle worker in you.

1) SPEAK IN FAITH.

The word of power is in your mouth, but it has no effect until you speak it. Remember, the Holy Spirit clothes Himself with you. He speaks with your mouth and tongue, transmitting His mighty power in your word, breath, and sound. His words become yours, and your words become His. Now your words carry His healing, deliverance, blessing, victory, and breakthrough power.

In my story at the beginning of this chapter, I spoke boldly in faith because I wanted the audience to be touched by God's power. I didn't know a satanist assigned to kill me was there. I did what I have done numerous times—speak what I wanted to happen. I didn't know what was going to happen, but I knew when I spoke, the Holy Spirit was going to do what I said. In this situation, I said, "Receive."

Those in the audience who were ready to receive from Him were going to be touched in all sorts of miraculous ways. When I said, "Touch of the Holy Spirit," people were touched with or without laying hands on them.

The miracle worker in you awaits you to unleash His movement and work. Whatever results you desire to see in the natural, speak it, and you will bring heaven's kingdom realities on Earth in the here and now.

2) ACT IN FAITH AND OBEDIENCE.

You unleash the Miracle Worker and His power within you through acts of faith and obedience. When the Holy Spirit says, "Anoint with oil and pray," do just that immediately. If He says, "Do communion and pray for your healing miracle," then do communion and pray. If you're ministering, and He says, "Wave your hand over the audience," then don't do anything different. If He leads you to raise your hand over the crowd and say, "The power of God is right where you are," then raise your hand and say that.

As you will read throughout this book, I received my healings, breakthroughs, and victories in my personal life and in ministry outreaches as a result of acting in faith and obedience to the Holy Spirit. You may think that you need someone more anointed to pray for you or someone with greater faith to believe with you. There are many great benefits from other people's anointing and faith. However, if you speak and act in faith and obedience to what the Holy Spirit speaks to you, then you'll find that your anointing and faith are as effective as any spiritual general in history for unleashing all kinds of miracles, signs, and wonders for you and for others.

THE DEVIL'S POWER IS NO MATCH FOR GOD'S UNLIMITED POWER

Now, I'll finish the story from the beginning of this chapter.

A week before the meeting that had the satanist assigned to kill me, I had an encounter with Jesus. I had just finished seven days of prayer and fasting and was getting ready to travel to Nairobi, Kenya, for this gospel crusade and conference.

The Lord said, "Andrew, ask me for a double portion."

"I beg your pardon," I responded. "A double portion of what, Lord?"

"Andrew, ask me for a double portion of my kingly anointing upon your life."

Not knowing what to expect with so many questions running through my head, I acted out of obedience to the still small but bold and authoritative voice in my spirit. So, I made the request. "Lord Jesus," I said, "please give me a double portion of your kingly anointing." I didn't feel, hear, and see anything afterward, but God had heard my simple prayer.

A week later, we traveled to Nairobi, Kenya. God knew I was going to encounter a satanist who could turn into all sorts of animals and creatures and objects. They call them "shapeshifters." This wasn't dealing with someone tormented or possessed by a demon. He was a satanic general in charge of other satanists in six countries. Within the church leadership, you can say he was a satanic bishop.

But God knew who else was coming and what their needs were. I needed a double portion of the kingly anointing of Jesus to triumph and have victory over the satanic assignment against my life and to see thousands saved, healed, and set free that day.

This satanist came to the crusade to kill the preacher, and I was that preacher. He had a ring on his finger with the demonic spirit of death. When He turned that ring toward his assignment, which happened to be me that day, he would release that demon of death that would cause me to collapse from a sudden heart attack and die. But that wasn't what happened. When he pointed the death ring at me, it didn't work. The demon of death couldn't touch me, let alone kill me. So, he started to make his way toward the pulpit.

I had taken the microphone and had the worship team sing "Oh, the Blood of Jesus." I invited everyone to stand and worship.

After the song, it was "go time" for power. I raised my right hand over the crowd, and with faith and authority in my voice, I proclaimed, "The power of God is right where you are."

The power of God was released through my words by faith. The satanist was stopped in his tracks.

Remember the week before, I had asked God for a double portion of Jesus's kingly anointing, and He gave it to me. Through the double portion of that anointing, there was greater activity, a greater demonstration of power of the Holy Spirit that was at work in me and through me. Also, there were greater manifestations of the miraculous signs and wonders.

It was too powerful to explain in words. God's power was so mighty that it took out one of Satan's generals and shifted the spiritual environment for that whole region that evening.

Only God knew that if I was going to triumph and overcome, be victorious in those meetings and accomplish His assignment, I didn't only need the kingly anointing, but I needed a double portion of His power operating in my life.

He was no match for the Holy Spirit. He got bombarded by God's power and was knocked out all night.

The next day, one of the pastors brought him for deliverance to the house where we were staying. I led him to the Lord and cast out over 45,000 demons that were in him. He got totally free in a matter of hours.

After deliverance, he told us the whole story and what he was commissioned to do when he came to our gathering. Up until that point, I had dealt with witches, warlocks, and devil worshippers of all ranks but not a shapeshifter.

I was in awe of God's love and power as I listened to his story. He's now a mighty preacher for the gospel of Jesus Christ. Glory to God!

GOD HAS NO FAVORITES

God isn't a respecter of persons. What He did for one, He will do for you as you speak and take the appropriate actions of faith and obedience.

> I now realize how true it is that God does not show favoritism. (See Acts 10:34, Romans 2:11, and Galatians 2:6.)

What will you believe God for today? Do you desire a touch of God in your life, marriage, children, loved ones, business, or ministry? Give something to the Holy Spirit to work with. He needs and waits for your works and action. Unleash the power of the Holy Spirit by speaking and acting in faith and obedience.

Now join me in the next chapter as I show you how to heal the sick.

CHAPTER 19
Heal the Sick

"YOU HAVE LOW THYROID or hypothyroidism, which means that your thyroid gland is not producing the thyroid hormones your body needs to regulate your energy, your appetite, and your metabolism. That's why you've been exercising, eating healthier than you ever have before, but you're still not able to lose weight and why your energy is very low. We're going to have to give you medication," the doctor explained.

I received this diagnosis in the fall of 2008, while living in Dallas and had launched a new church. Lethargy overwhelmed me as I tried to meet the demands of running a church and everything else in my life. My energy level didn't feel the same.

I met the demands, but not without a struggle and consumption of energy drinks, energy bars, energy smoothies, and lots of coffee, none of which were good for me. I even worked out at the gym three to five days a week hoping to bring my energy levels up, but that didn't help either. Regardless of my efforts, I would get so tired that by 2:00 in the afternoon, I had to go home and take a nap to rejuvenate me to finish the day.

I went to a doctor for a checkup to see what was going on. The doctor ran a bunch of tests on me over the next several days, including extensive blood work. A couple of weeks later, I went back to the doctor's office for the results. The diagnosis was low thyroid or hypothyroidism.

After explaining to me what that meant, he proceeded to write a script for me to take to the pharmacy for the medication he said I would have to take for the rest of my life.

Two weeks after starting the medication, I went back to see the doctor. Because I wasn't experiencing much improvement, he increased the dosage so I could become somewhat functional. As I drove back from that doctor's visit, I asked, "God is this it? Is this real? What do You want me to do?"

The Lord responded, "Believe Me. I'm the Lord, your Healer."

Before I share with you how my miracle healing unfolded, let me walk you through what the Bible says about sickness and disease and how to heal the sick. If we're going to receive divine healing, wholeness, and freedom from oppression, first we need to know what sickness and disease are.

SICKNESS AND DISEASE ARE CAPTIVITY.

So Satan went from the presence of the Lord and afflicted Job with painful sores from the soles of his feet to the crown of his head (Job 2:7 NIV).

And the Lord turned the captivity of Job, when he prayed for his friends . . . (Job 42:10).

Did you make the connection? Job was sick, and the Lord turned his captivity by healing his sickness when he prayed for his friends. Sickness is captivity according to the Bible.

SICKNESS AND DISEASE ARE BONDAGE.

"So ought not this woman, being a daughter of Abraham, whom Satan has bound—think of it—for eighteen years, be loosed from this bond on the Sabbath?" (Luke 13:16).

I don't think or believe that God is going to put His children under bondage just so He can teach them a lesson. According to the Bible, sickness is captivity, and sickness is bondage.

In the above Scripture of Luke 13:16, Jesus was talking to those religious people who were accusing Him of healing this woman on the Sabbath Day. What bound her was the spirit of infirmity.

SICKNESS AND DISEASE ARE OPPRESSION.

how God anointed Jesus of Nazareth with the Holy Spirit and with great power; and He went around doing good and healing all who were oppressed by the devil, because God was with Him (Acts 10:38 AMP).

We can clearly see in the verse above that sickness and disease are oppression. I want to point out this reality that at the **source of every sickness and disease is the spirit of infirmity from Satan**. He attacks a person's body, mind, and emotions.

As God created man, He gave them the breath of life through the spirit of life. But Satan comes to steal, kill, and destroy. (See John 10:10.) He brings death and has a spirit that gives demonic life to sickness and diseases, such as cancer, to attack God's people. If there is infirmity, there is a demonic life in it.

That's why as we seek healing for ourselves and for others, we exercise the seven methods to unleash healing miracles out of our bodies.

STEP 1: IDENTIFY THE EVIL SPIRIT BEHIND THE SICKNESS OR DISEASE.

How do you identify that evil spirit? If you're ministering to somebody, ask them. If they don't know what it is, observe that person and listen for the discernment and perception from the Holy Spirit.

As you're following these methods, consistently depend on the Holy Spirit at each stage. He'll show you and help you, but you must first identify the spirit behind the sickness or the oppression so that your prayer can be effective.

IDENTIFY THE RULING SPIRIT: Find the medical term for the afflicted person's condition, and then give it a biblical term. The "woman who was bent over" was given the biblical term "spirit of infirmity" (Luke 13:11–12).

For example, the medical specialist may say that you have glaucoma or cataracts, but Jesus said, "It is the blind spirit." Go after the blind spirit. You speak. Use the authority of the name and release your faith.

If you're ministering to a multitude, raise your hands, pray over the crowd, and start rebuking the spirits by name. You'll see that after casting out that infirmity, that sick person gets healed most of the time.

The spirit of infirmity is a personality. You can't rebuke anything that doesn't understand your words. You can only rebuke a personality because the personality understands your words.

When evening had come, they brought unto him many that were possessed with devils: and he cast out the spirits with his word, and healed all that were sick: (Matthew 8:16).

Here is something I want you to note: the verse above says that the people who were sick, who were brought to Jesus, were possessed by devils.

Now that gives us a clue that devils were the cause of their sickness. He casts out devils and healed them.

Do you now see the connection between sickness, disease, and devils? The people who were brought to Jesus were afflicted by some type of demon. Then when He cast out a demon, that sick person got healed.

Let me also point out that not all sick people are possessed by devils. They are oppressed by devils behind the sickness or disease.

DIFFERENT SPIRITS BUT SAME DEVIL: There are different kinds of demons, unclean spirits, or evil spirits just like there are many different types of people. Jesus cast out devils that were oppressing the people. We're going to follow His example. Again, we're using the same method, the same way Jesus did it, the same way the apostles did it, and we're going to see the same results they did. We only have to believe in what we're doing and who sent us to do what we're doing. Let us look at a few examples.

How did Jesus heal the bent-over woman? The medical term would be "handicapped" or "disabled," but the biblical term is the "spirit of infirmity."

Let's look at it here in Luke 13:11–12: "And behold, there was a woman who had the spirit of infirmity . . ." First, the Bible reveals the ruling spirit and what caused her to be bent over for eighteen years— the spirit of infirmity and that she could in no way raise herself up. But when Jesus saw her, He called her to Him and said, **"Woman, you are loosed from your infirmity**." In other words, He cast out the spirit of infirmity that caused her to be bent over. She was instantly healed.

Healing of the Deaf and Dumb Boy:

When Jesus saw that the people came running together, He rebuked the unclean spirit, saying to it, "Deaf and dumb spirit, I command you, come out of him and enter him no more!" (Mark 9:25).

Now do you see how simple this is? As in the biblical days, so it is today. As we discussed earlier, every sickness and disease have a spirit of infirmity behind it that's giving it life. It's an evil life that oppresses, torments, and plagues God's people. In the case in the previous Scripture, it was the deaf and dumb spirit. This person could not talk.

It's the same today. Cast that spirit out. Call it by name—deaf and dumb spirit. Jesus commanded it, and it came out. That's the same way you and I can do it.

Healing of the Dumb Man:

As they went out, behold, they brought to Him a man, mute and demon possessed (Matthew 9:32).

Again, there was a spirit behind that man's inability to speak. When you find somebody who can't speak, love on them by administering the power of God to them. When you rebuke that spirit in the name of Jesus, their tongue is loosed, that spirit leaves, and that person can speak. This is how Jesus did it, and you and I can do it too.

And when the demon was cast out, the mute spoke. And the multitudes marveled, saying, "It was never seen like this in Israel!" (Matthew 9:33).

In Luke 4:33–35, a man in a synagogue was set free from an unclean spirit. ". . . And he [unclean spirit] cried out with a loud voice, saying, 'Let us alone!' . . . But Jesus rebuked him, saying, 'Be quiet, and come out of him!' . . ." Do you see how Jesus did it? Speak the Word, and use His authority.

Continuing with Luke 4:35, ". . . And when the demon had thrown him in their midst, it came out of him and did not hurt him."

This was a rebellious spirit. I've seen them where somebody wants to talk during the service or cause chaos. With one word, you command them to be quiet and the spirit to come out. Jesus did it in His meeting, and we can use the same model. You don't have to take them to another room and spend hours with them behind closed doors. No, that's when you don't know your authority. But when you know your authority, you speak.

Sometimes you may lay hands on the person and anoint them with oil. Certainly, do so if the Spirit leads you to do that. But we are talking about a new spiritual breakthrough where you can begin to pray without laying hands, without anointing with oil. You are ready in whatever situation you find yourself!

Healing of the Blind and Dumb Man:

Then a demon-possessed man—he was both blind and unable to talk—was brought to Jesus, and Jesus healed him so that he could both speak and see (Matthew 12:22 TLB).

Healing from a Fever:

But Simon's wife's mother lay sick with a fever, and they told Him about her at once. So He came and took her by the hand and lifted her up, and immediately the fever left her. And she served them (Mark 1:30–31).

This is the method of laying on of hands in action. Jesus knew His authority. He took her by the hand, and she was healed instantly.

We see Peter and John at the gate of the temple called "Beautiful" in Acts 3:1–8. As they went to pray, a crippled man asked them for alms. They said, "In the name of Jesus, rise up and walk." In this instance, Peter didn't even pray.

Mark 16:17–18, tells us that if we'll lay hands on the sick, they'll recover. Why? Because in you is the anointing. When you come into contact with somebody who needs that anointing, it begins to flow. You have to believe you can, because if you don't, then you can't. Allow yourself to be God's vessel.

Step 2: Project Yourself by an Act of Faith in the Spirit.

Project yourself into the spirit world by an act of faith as you confront every spirit of infirmity that has tormented, plagued, or pressed you or God's people. You exercise your spiritual authority in the Spirit when you speak and act.

STEP 3: REBUKE, ADJURE, AND CAST OUT THOSE SPIRITS IN THE NAME OF JESUS TO COME OUT AND LEAVE FOREVER.

That's right. You rebuke, cast out, adjure, or command those spirits to leave forever in the name of Jesus. Most of the time when we cast out spirits, the Bible tells us in Matthew 12:44–45 and Luke 11:24–26 that "they go and wander, and if they don't find a place to rest, they're going to come back." Command them to go and not to return anymore.

STEP 4: USE THE METHODS OF MINISTERING GOD'S POWER TO HEAL THE SICK AND CAST OUT THE SPIRIT.

Basically, as you're rebuking, you're using one or more methods of unleashing miracles to minister God's power to heal the sick and cast out demons:

- Speaking the Word in faith and authority
- Exercising your delegated authority in Christ
- Exercising your faith in God's promises
- Laying on of hands
- Anointing with oil
- Having holy communion
- Seeking God's miracle healing strategy

This is how I did it, and it's been several years now since God gave me a new thyroid.

When laying on of hands, I applied the blood of Jesus, anointed myself with oil, and I prayed at my house. You can pray something like this:

In the name of Jesus Christ of Nazareth, spirit of infirmity, I cast you out of my thyroid gland. Come out of it through the blood of Jesus Christ and return no more. Amen.

You see how simple that was? When you speak and release the authority and the power of Jesus, you see great wonders from God for you and for others.

If somebody with glaucoma or cataracts in their eyes are losing their eyesight, this is the prayer you can pray right now:

You blind spirit, I command you in the mighty name of Jesus Christ to come out of his or her eyes and return no more. I release the healing life of Jesus Christ to manifest in his or her eyes. Thank you, Jesus for Your authority to heal the sick and cast out demons. Thank you, Lord, for healing him/her from blindness. I now cover his/her eyesight with Your precious blood. Amen.

STEP 5: RELEASE THE HEALING POWER OF THE HOLY SPIRIT ON THE PERSON OR ON YOURSELF.

Release the healing power of the Holy Spirit on the people or yourself.

STEP 6: THANK GOD FOR HIS AUTHORITY TO HEAL THE SICK AND CAST OUT DEMONS AFTER YOU HAVE CAST THEM OUT.

You see you have cast out the spirit. Now you are praying for the healing power to perfect that miracle, to fill their lives, and permeate their whole body until they are perfectly healed and delivered and set free. You may pray something like this:

Heavenly Father, in the name of Jesus Christ, Your Son, I ask for the miracle healing power of Jesus to permeate him, her, or everyone until they are perfectly healed by the anointing and the presence of Jesus in their lives. Thank you, Jesus, for Your authority to heal the sick and cast out demons. Amen.

Step 7: Thank God for Answering Prayer.

Again, you are releasing your faith. You're thanking God for answering prayer. Lead the person or persons in thanksgiving for God's healing power that's touching their lives right there. You go from petitioning to receiving the miracle by faith.

Step 8: Encourage Them to Put Their Faith into Action.

While they continue giving thanks to God for the healing power that's touching their lives, encourage them to put their faith into action. Ask them to do something they could not previously do. If they're lame, command them to get up and walk in the name of Jesus. If they can't see, tell them to open their eyes and receive their sight in the name of Jesus.

We use the name of Jesus at every turn because saying His name brings the active presence of His life, power, and reality into our time, space, and position in the here and now.

HOW MY THYROID HEALING MANIFESTED

I have ministered healing miracles, signs, and wonders to other people, but I was desperate for my own. I made a choice to stop the prescription medication for my thyroid disorder and use natural remedies. I was doing what I could as I sought God's strategy.

I knew I had heard from God to believe Him. I asked God what He wanted me to do.

During the process of seeking His healing strategy, the Lord sent us to do missionary work in Europe for a few years. While there, one of our missionary friends had the same problem with low thyroid. She shared her supplements with me, and they helped.

Then one night in 2011, three years after my initial hypothyroidism diagnosis, I was praying in our apartment in Timisoara, Romania. The anointing was in me and upon me, but I hadn't really tapped into the potential of this anointing for my own healing. I was releasing it to everybody else but me.

One morning at four o'clock, I was praying in the living room, pacing back and forth. "Okay, Lord, what is the secret to accessing the anointing within and upon me?" I asked. "Show me the secret."

Suddenly, I heard the Holy Spirit say, "I want you to receive it through the blood. I want you to use the blood and release the anointing for healing. Don't pray for healing. Ask me for a new thyroid gland."

Immediately, I laid my hands at the base of my neck where my thyroid gland was located, and I applied the blood of Jesus. I released the power of God to create a new thyroid gland. I declared, and I spoke a new thyroid gland into being in the name of Jesus by the anointing of the Holy Spirit. And God did it.

I went back to the doctors. They checked my thyroid, and it was perfect. I went back again, and they rechecked it. Still, my thyroid was perfect. I went back a few months later and many more times over a period of two years, and each time they ran tests on my thyroid, the results showed it was perfect.

We moved from Romania to the United Kingdom for our ministry to be better located for traveling in Europe. I went to a doctor there, and he confirmed my thyroid was perfect. When we returned to the United States, I went back to the doctor, and the doctor confirmed yet again that my thyroid was perfect. Since late 2011, God miraculously recreated my thyroid gland through the anointing that was already in me.

Nobody laid hands on me. Through the anointing, I received a brand spanking new thyroid gland. So, if you need a miracle, you can release the anointing.

In this book, I am showing you how you can release the anointing. You can have other people pray for you, but you don't need to have other people pray for you all the time. Those anointed to pray for you or have faith for what you believe aren't going to always pray for you. So, believe for yourself, and God will use your faith. Just have faith in your own faith.

In my instance, I had faith for a lot of people, but perhaps I didn't have the faith for my own situation, not until the Holy Spirit gave me His strategy. Remember, faith comes by hearing and hearing by the word of the Lord (Romans 10:17).

If you need a miracle, it's not beyond your reach. The anointing is in you and upon you. Just allow yourself to flow with the Holy Spirit. He's going to help you. He's going to lead you. He knows the key to your healing or for the person to whom you are ministering.

Let's continue exploring our keys and the power of each as I take you into the next chapter to teach you about casting out demons and setting the captives free.

CHAPTER 20

Cast Out Demons and Set the Captives Free

A CHRISTIAN COUPLE, who had a heart to reach people in their region, invited me to speak in a small Idaho town for a whole week of power and miracles. Though they weren't professional preachers, they felt a call from God to build a three-hundred seat hall to invite ministers to hold meetings where people in their community and nearby areas could get saved and set free.

They also invited another couple from San Diego, California, to speak and do praise and worship. This couple drove their whole family from California to Idaho.

One of their children was a young woman I'll call Beth. They had met Beth while working in their ministry in California, and they adopted her.

Beth was probably twenty-one years old at this time with medium built, about five feet five inches tall, heavily tattooed, and had a quiet and serious demeanor. During these services, she sat in the outside seat in middle aisle so that she could better see and hear the preacher.

For several days, I preached and invited people to get saved. Then I would proceed to pray for miracles of healing and deliverance.

Beth's face remained expressionless, yet the rest of the audience shouted for joy when somebody received a miracle. But God was working in Beth's heart. She had been through so much in her young life—sexual abuse and satanic ritual abuse that involved several forms of demonic worship, sacrifices, and initiations. One can only imagine what she had been through. Perhaps that explains why she kept to herself and was very skeptical and hesitant to open up to people, even to God.

But on the fourth day, I preached a short message on the power of the blood of Jesus and invited people to receive Jesus Christ as their Lord and Savior. To my surprise, Beth walked right up to the altar. It was as if she was waiting for me to make the call.

After praying a prayer of surrender to Christ with those who had come forward, I invited the sick and the oppressed to come forward. Beth stayed at the altar for prayer. She showed no signs of demonic oppression until I went to pray for her.

Suddenly, all the demons began manifesting. She couldn't look me in the eye when I asked her what she wanted prayer for. With a surge of demonic strength, she threw down two strong adult men who stood beside her to catch her so she wouldn't fall down when God's power touched her.

At that point, I took a step back and observed her. I listened to the Holy Spirit for discernment and revelation.

Before I tell you what happened next, let me take you through the steps of casting out demons and setting the captives free. Then I'll come back and finish this amazing deliverance story of this young woman.

STEPS FOR EFFECTIVE DELIVERANCE

In the previous chapter, Chapter 19, we talked about healing the sick. We discovered how the source of sickness and disease is the spirit of infirmity that's from Satan. It's that demonic or satanic life that attacks

God's people through their bodies, minds, and emotions. In this chapter, we're going to look at the cause, the root of oppression, bondage, and infirmity.

The spirit of infirmity and any other demons are personalities. That's why we can cast them out, rebuke them, and they obey because they understand when you address them in the name of Jesus. You can't rebuke anything that doesn't understand your words. You can only rebuke a personality.

Jesus cast out demons by words. Let us follow His way. That's how we do it. That's how I've been doing it for the last thirty years, and you'll be doing it the same way if you haven't already started.

If this is all new to you, though, then how do you cast out demons effectively? It's essentially the same procedure as healing but slightly different in that now, we want to identify the strong man, the ruling demon spirit or evil personality that's tormenting that person. Jesus always looked for that strong man.

If you're starting to learn this process or want to do self-deliverance, follow these steps that are similar to the steps given in the previous chapter regarding healing the sick. You can go through them in the same order I suggest, or you can follow the Holy Spirit as He prompts you. Remember every situation is different.

STEP 1: ASK THE PERSON QUESTIONS REGARDING THE TORMENTING.

You can ask the person you're ministering deliverance to if they know what's tormenting them, when the torment started, and what provokes it. If they don't know for sure, then go to step two.

STEP 2: OBSERVE THE TORMENTED PERSON, AND LISTEN TO THE HOLY SPIRIT TALK TO YOU ABOUT THEM.

Watch the tormented person and listen to the Holy Spirit. He will give you discernment or perception of what is tormenting them if the person doesn't know. He'll also show you who the strong man is and why he's there. We need to be flexible and do what the Holy Spirit says.

Mark 3:26–27 says, "And if Satan has risen up against himself, and is divided, he cannot stand, but has an end. No one can enter a strong man's house and plunder his goods, unless he first binds the strong man. And then he will plunder his house."

If you're going to do deliverance on somebody who is demon-possessed or heavily tormented by demons, you need to know who the strong man in charge of the other little demons in that person is.

I don't waste time with the little lieutenants. I want the general. Don't waste your time with the little demons. Those are the ones you first encounter. Cast them out, and go for the general. That's the way Jesus does it. He goes for the strong man, the general.

STEP 3: COMMAND THE UNCLEAN SPIRIT TO IDENTIFY ITSELF IF NEED BE.

Let's see how Jesus did it.

> And he cried out with a loud voice and said, "What have I to do with You, Jesus, Son of the Most High God? I implore You by God that You do not torment me." For He said to him, "Come out of the man, unclean spirit!" Then He asked him, "What *is* your name? . . ." (Mark 5:7–9).

Here, Jesus asked the demon to identify itself. Most of the time, they identify themselves first, but when they don't and I need to know, then just like Jesus, I ask.

In the previous passage, the unclean spirit answered Jesus's question. ". . . And he answered, saying, 'My name *is* Legion; for we are many'" (Mark 5:9–10).

But here is caution. When you ask, remember Satan is a liar. Depend on the Holy Spirit to witness if that is the demon's real name because they may play with you, lie to you, especially if your discernment isn't very strong. You have to be in the Spirit and allow the Holy Spirit to give you that discernment. We see that Jesus did it, so we need to take His lead.

STEP 4: CALL IT AN UNCLEAN SPIRIT.

If you can't identify the strong man, then call it as Jesus did before He asked Legion to identify itself. He called it an unclean spirit, foul spirit, or evil spirit.

As I've stated earlier, it's necessary to know the identity because it's a personality you're dealing with. The person from whom you're casting it out is now going to be free.

STEP 5: PROJECT YOURSELF BY AN ACT OF FAITH OUT INTO THE SPIRIT WORLD.

Project yourself by faith into the spirit where you confront every spirit of infirmity, of bondage, and of oppression that has tormented, afflicted, or oppressed you or other people to whom you're ministering. This is where we exercise our authority in the spirit.

Whether I'm doing individual deliverance or in a big service or mass crusade, this is what I do—project myself into the spirit world. As a result, I see demons come out of many people immediately.

STEP 6: REBUKE, CAST OUT, ADJURE THE STRONG MAN.

In Matthew 8:28–29, Jesus was in the region of Gadarenes when "... two demon possessed men coming from the tombs met him. They were so violent that no one could pass that way. 'What do you want with us, Son of God?' they shouted. 'Have you come here to torture us before the appointed time?'" (NIV).

What time was the demon talking about? It was talking about the time of judgment. That's why when you're casting out demons, you're not judging the demons. You're commanding them to come out and to return no more. Even the demons know their time to be judged has not yet come.

STEP 7: USE THE METHODS OF UNLEASHING MIRACLES TO CAST OUT DEMONS.

We will cover the methods of unleashing miracles in Chapter 22 "Release Signs, Miracles, and Wonders Using Biblical Methods." Use those methods. Speak.

Take your authority, and command it. Jesus cast out demons by a word. You and I do the same. Use your authority in Jesus.

I've dealt with some stubborn spirits that don't want to come out and leave. Then I used the blood of Jesus. Use the power of the blood. Walk in the authority God has given you to use Jesus's name. Believe in yourself and that you are God's partner, His representative, and that He is in you and with you.

That's how you release the power. Sometimes, you may lay hands on people.

As you activate the power of the kingdom in you, you'll grow in authority and power and find that you don't even need to lay hands on people. You could raise your hand or point your finger and cast the demons out. Be led by the Spirit. If He leads you to lay hands, don't point your finger; lay hands. If He leads you to anoint them with oil and pray, do just that.

But what if you don't have a specific sensing from the Holy Spirit? Then just go and use all the methods like I've laid out in Chapter 22.

For example, you could say, "Legion, I command you in the name of Jesus of Nazareth to come out of this man or woman now and return no more."

It's that simple. You have the anointing. You exercise your authority, you speak, and you release the power.

Sometimes demons resist, surrendering and leaving immediately like this particular demon that Jesus was dealing with in Mark 5:7–13. Jesus was in control, even though He was talking to this demon.

You too have the authority to send them wherever God says you need to send them. That could be to the dry land or the bottomless pit. You can lock them there with a judgment key of Christ until the day of judgment.

WHEN DEMONS REFUSE TO COME OUT BECAUSE OF ITS LEGAL RIGHTS: Almost always, satanic rituals, occults, and devil worship involve blood sacrifices of animals and birds during initiations and establishing satanic covenants, contracts, and allegiance.

As a result, these demonic spirits don't want to leave those they inhabit, like in the story of the young woman you'll read about at the end of this chapter.

What do you do when demons refuse to leave because of the blood ritual covenant or an initiation, a sacrifice when they were invited? Simple. Give them the blood of Jesus. The blood removes the legal right that Satan has on them by nullifying all of those satanic contracts, covenants, and allegiances.

I've dealt with witches, warlocks, and shapeshifters deep into satanism and operating at the highest levels in demonology and witchcraft. I saw them get saved and delivered. Because most of the satanic occults and devil worship involve blood sacrifices, getting them set free has always involved the blood of Christ.

STEP 8: THANK GOD FOR HIS AUTHORITY TO CAST OUT DEMONS.

Always give thanks to God for the authority and power to cast out demons. Also, thank Him for the miracle of deliverance that has just occurred.

STEP 9: FILL THE EMPTY HOUSE WITH THE SPIRIT OF GOD.

After you have done deliverance, fill the empty house with the Spirit of God.

> When the unclean spirit is gone out of a man, he walketh through dry places, seeking rest, and findeth none. Then he saith, I will return into my house from whence I came out; and when he is come, he findeth it empty, swept, and garnished. Then goeth he, and taketh with himself seven other spirits more wicked than himself, and they enter in

and dwell there: and the last state of that man is worse than the first. Even so shall it be also unto this wicked generation (Matthew 12:43–45).

Now that the evil spirit has been cast out, this person needs to be filled with the Spirit of God, who will saturate that individual with the life of Jesus Christ. Pray for the person to be filled with God's Spirit. If they have already received the baptism in the Holy Spirit, then pray for them to be refilled, to overflow with the Spirit and the power of God.

If you need guidance on how to minister to them or have yourself filled with the Holy Spirit, see Chapter 8 "The Baptism in the Holy Spirit Key." Here is a simple example prayer:

Dear Heavenly Father, in the name of Jesus Christ, Your Son, I ask You to fill this person, his whole heart, mind, soul, emotions, intellect, will, and body with the fullness of Your life and power until they are perfectly filled and saturated by the anointing and the presence of Jesus in their lives from this moment on. Amen.

STEP 10: THANK GOD FOR THAT ANSWERED PRAYER.

Lead the person into thanksgiving for deliverance and for God's power that is at work in their life.

STEP 11: ENCOURAGE THEM TO LIVE A GODLY LIFESTYLE.

Exhort that person who has just gotten delivered to live a lifestyle of prayer, of holiness, faith in God, and love. Why? When the enemy comes to live in the house, it's occupied. There's a new sheriff in town, and He's Jesus Christ through the person of the Holy Spirit.

As I finish this chapter, I want to give you a word of caution not to start casting out demons if you need deliverance yourself. Either seek deliverance first from others or use the methods and steps in the next chapter on how to minister deliverance and healing to yourself.

After you've been delivered, then go deliver others. But if you don't need deliverance of any kind, then I encourage you to allow Jesus to use you to deliver and set the captives free.

HOW BETH GOT
TOTALLY DELIVERED IN MINUTES

Now, let's get back to the story from the beginning of this chapter so I can tell you about Beth's deliverance.

I then heard the Lord say, "She has forty-thousand demons in her head." He then opened my spiritual eyes, and I could see how and where these demons were connected to her mind and the rest her body. It was go-time for deliverance.

The Holy Spirit led me to move my hand over her head, unwrapping the black tape that I had seen over her mind that represented the spirit of deception. She manifested even more, kicking and shaking her head uncontrollably for several minutes while I cast out every demon spirit in her mind.

When those were gone, the Holy Spirit said, "Twenty-thousand demons are left." Then I moved to the ones connected to her neck and spine. As I laid one of my hands on her neck, she began to cough and shake violently for several minutes. They too came out.

The Holy Spirit said, "Now, ten-thousand are left."

I told her to put her hand on her belly button. Trembling, she did what I said, and I commanded every demon spirit connected to her belly button to loose her and come out in the name of Jesus.

Suddenly, she began to vomit all kinds of stuff including dark green and blue fluids. To say it was gross is a big understatement. The ushers couldn't find a bucket for her to vomit into fast enough.

A few minutes after those demons left, she calmed down and stopped shaking and vomiting. I thought it was done.

The Spirit said, "Four more are left."

I commanded the ruling spirit or the strong man and all his helpers that had been controlling her life to come out in the name of Jesus.

At that time, this beautiful woman's countenance changed to that of a warrior and one with authority. Her voice also changed. She looked me in the eyes and demanded blood, saying, "I was given blood when I was invited to come into her. I need blood if I'm going to leave her."

I said, "That's fine. I'll give you the blood."

When I started this deliverance, I had applied the blood over her. I knew there was going to be some intense manifestations as the strong man and its cohorts left the young woman. Thankfully, I had four of my own strong men from the church standing beside her so that she wouldn't be thrown down by the demon or hurt in any way.

THE STRONG MAN LEAVES

Then I said, "In the name of Jesus Christ, I give you the blood of Jesus Christ."

As soon as those words came out of my mouth, she began to scream, shake, and jump as if she wanted to run away, but our four men held her in one place.

The strong man in her screamed, "Oh no, not that blood! Not that blood! I don't want that blood!"

The more the demon yelled it didn't want it, the more I said, "I give you the blood of Jesus Christ." Then I added, "I cancel any agreement, covenant, contract, initiation that was made by her or on her behalf by other people knowingly and unknowingly. I nullify your authority now and any legal right you have on her. She now belongs to Jesus. She is not your property anymore."

Oh, my goodness. I had four big men holding this young lady. When I said, "You foul spirit, come out along with your helpers and leave her now. She is now the property of Jesus," the strong man and his demonic helpers staged one last assault to try to hurt her. They welled up in her and threw her and the four men holding her down, and then they left. Thankfully no one was hurt.

When they were gone, she let out a big sigh. It was if she had just finished a big battle or ran a marathon. In all honesty, she had. She was free at last—completely set free by the power of God!

She stood up, thanked me, and went back to her seat. Talk about fighting. I'm glad I was there to help her in that fight. The people cheered, praised God, and worshipped Him.

The next day, she danced and praised with complete abandonment, thanking God for setting her free. During the prayer time, she came forward and got baptized in the Holy Spirit. As I prayed over her, the Lord gave me a prophetic word about her future, family, and destiny.

A few years ago, she emailed me to tell me about how God had fulfilled everything I had prophesied over her that day. God had given her the husband I had describe, and now they were married and had a powerful missionary ministry in Mexico, which was another fulfillment of that prophesy. They wanted to thank me again for ministering to her and helping her get delivered.

We give praise, honor, and all the glory to God. I want you to use these steps as you're starting out. If you're a veteran, I pray that you're being empowered to go to the next level.

If you need to experience healing or deliverance in your own body, join me in the next chapter where I will show you how to minister to yourself.

CHAPTER 21

Minister Healing and Deliverance to Yourself

"ASK ME HOW I AM HEALING YOU?"

"Lord, how are you healing me?" I asked.

This was the third time the Lord told me to ask Him this question. Like me, you were probably taught not to ask God how He was doing something; you just believe. But my personal relationship with the Lord has shown me that He wants me to know, to understand what He's doing and how He's doing it. Sometimes, He'll reveal why.

This recent interaction was in June 2018. I had gone to the doctor for a regular checkup. An hour later, I was diagnosed with type 2 diabetes. My blood sugar was 560, and my hemoglobin A1C was 10.90. I needed immediate intervention.

My physician told me he had sent a prescription to my pharmacy for insulin and other medication to help my body with my diabetes. He instructed me that while there, I would need to purchase insulin pens for the injections, a glucometer, specialized needles to prick my finger, and test strips.

I couldn't believe what was happening. I listened to my physician in utter surprise! *How did I get here?* I wondered! I wasn't obese.

"What's the cause of this?" I asked.

The doctor shrugged. "Could be from genetics, a bad diet, or other factors. We don't know exactly."

When I came out the doctor's office, I sat in my car for a while. *I'll send out the prayer request to our partners to pray with me*, I thought.

Suddenly I heard that still small voice in my spirit. "Believe in your faith. Don't email anyone. Have faith in your faith."

So many thoughts ran through my mind. My life had changed. My doctor told me to accept the diabetes as my portion for the rest of my life.

Still sitting in my car, I again heard the Lord say, "I am going to heal you, but I want you to ask me how I am healing you."

"Lord, how are you healing me?" I asked quietly.

He revealed His miracle strategy, which I'll share with you at the end of this chapter.

At ten o'clock that evening, my physician's office left two voicemails instructing me to go to the emergency room. They had taken blood for further tests, and the results were not good. They were concerned that something bad would happen if the high blood sugar was not controlled immediately in a setting where I could be monitored.

I didn't see the missed calls until the next day. I listened to the voice messages but didn't go to the emergency room. Instead, I called my physician, and he asked me to come in to see him. He saw that I was functioning and could go on with my usual daily life.

So, how did my healing unfold?

Let me walk you through the steps on how to minister healing and deliverance to yourself. Then I'll come back and show you how my healing manifested.

STEP 1: IDENTIFY YOUR CONDITION.

Give your condition a biblical term, just like I instructed in Chapter 19 "Heal the Sick." If you can't find the name of your condition in the Bible, then call it by a name you know. For example, if you have glaucoma or cataracts, Jesus called it a blind spirit. If you have arthritis, the Bible calls it the spirit of infirmity.

Are you getting the idea? Address the spirit by its name because that is the demonic or satanic life of that disease or sickness you have.

STEP 2: REMIND YOURSELF WHAT GOD HAS PROMISED TO DO.

After you identify the ruling spirit behind your condition, come in agreement with God's promise as the basis of your faith. Christ died for more than our sins. What has Christ done for you to practice and claim that healing?

> He was despised and rejected by men, a man of *deep* sorrows who was no stranger to suffering and grief. We hid our faces from him in disgust and considered him a nobody, not worthy of respect. Yet he was the one who carried our sicknesses and endured the torment of our sufferings. We viewed him as one who was being punished for something he himself had done, as one who was struck down by God and brought low. But it was because of our rebellious deeds that he was pierced and because of our sins that he was crushed. He endured the punishment that made us completely whole, and in his wounding we found our healing (Isaiah 53:3–5 TPT).

For example, if you need a healing miracle, you may take God's promise in the Scripture above and personalize it, make it your own. If you're like me, when I want the truth to get deeper into my spirit man, I read the Bible out loud. Faith comes by hearing and hearing by the

Word of God. Try it. Read God's promises out loud. Let your ears hear the Word. Claim it. *It will build your faith.*

By doing so, you are assimilating and consuming the Word. You are aligning your faith and getting in agreement with what God is saying.

> "Behold, I give you the authority to trample on serpents and scorpions, and over all the power of the enemy, and nothing shall by any means hurt you" (Luke 10:19).

I found some believers who were afraid of trampling on the enemy because of his retaliation. Dear friend, whether you do it or not, he's already beating you up. You might as well exercise your authority and go on the offensive.

You see, when we play defense and lay back and wait, we think maybe it'll get better.

No! The devil is not going to have mercy on you.

God has given you the authority. Come in agreement with Him, and take that authority. Believe it, and then begin to act like it. You can't act like it if you don't believe it.

STEP 3: ACTIVATE HEALING AND DELIVERANCE IN YOUR LIFE THROUGH PRAYER.

You may anoint yourself with oil and pray. Unless the Holy Spirit is leading you to do it a certain way, I encourage you to just follow those methods. They're biblical.

> And they cast out many demons, and anointed with oil many who were sick, and healed *them* (Mark 6:13).

In Chapter 3 "Why You Need the Power of God," I shared a story about an epileptic boy. At that time, the Holy Spirit said, "Anoint with oil and pray."

Now, the power is not in the oil. The power is released because of your obedience and your faith to the promise of God's Word.

Do whatever Jesus tells you to do. I put some oil on this boy in the name of Jesus, but then I went after the spirit itself, the demon of epilepsy, the spirit of infirmity manifesting in epilepsy. Then I commanded it to pack its bags with all its friends and cast them all out and sent them into the abyss. Tell them where to go. Lock them up with the judgment key of Christ, and tell them not to come back anymore in Jesus's mighty name.

So here is an example:

In the name of Jesus Christ of Nazareth, spirit of infirmity, I cast you out of my pancreas. Come out of my pancreas through the blood of Jesus and return no more.

If you're losing hearing, that's a spirit of deafness. Command the spirit of infirmity or the deaf spirit that's attacking your hearing to come out through the blood of Jesus now and return no more in Jesus's mighty name.

Do you see how simple that is? You're addressing; you're not guessing. You are specific, and you're cursing out the personality that is giving life to that pain, to that sickness, to that disease you're encountering.

Here's another prayer. You're beginning to lose your eyesight. You know the doctor may say it's a degenerative sight disease or glaucoma. Call it what it is. Jesus called it the blind spirit. Call it the blind spirit, and if you don't know, call it the spirit of infirmity. Say,

You blind spirit, I command/cast/rebuke you out of my eyes. Come out and return no more in the name of Jesus Christ.

As you activate your faith by speaking, the power of God is transmitted through your words. Do that, and you're going to begin to see God at work.

I also shared the creative miracle story of my liver in Chapter 4 "The Blood of Jesus Christ—The Most Powerful of All Keys." Don't be shy in asking and believing God for creative miracles.

The Holy Spirit said, "Andrew, you have access by the blood. Use it. Don't ask for healing of your liver. Ask for a new one." Why ask for a repair when you can have a brand-new one, right?

Most of the time, we're praying for healing, but God actually wants us to have new body parts. I understand healing is scriptural, but God may want you to experience something new. As a matter of fact, I've seen people who had been blind receive new eyesight after the spirit of blindness was cast out. They have new eyes and new body parts. The power of God is going to invade and release His life in that part of your body or your whole being.

Can you imagine anybody who creates something they can't fix? Well, God created you, so He can fix you. He has the body parts to fix you. He's your Creator. He is your manufacturer, so to speak. Ask for a new liver.

Hebrews 4:16 says, "Let us therefore come boldly to the throne of grace, that we may obtain mercy and find grace to help in time of need."

I prayed the following prayer word for word for my creative miracle. I want you to see and know how simple it can be.

Dear Heavenly Father, I enter Your throne room through the shed blood of Jesus Christ, Your Son, asking You to take out my bad liver and replace it with a brand-spanking new one. In Jesus's name I pray, amen.

Instantly a creative miracle happened. You have the same access to receive creative miracles and healing or deliverance for yourself.

STEP 4: RELEASE THE HEALING POWER OF THE HOLY SPIRIT ON YOURSELF.

Release the healing power of the Spirit on yourself. Sometimes when I pray for myself and God's power falls on me, it goes through my body like a consuming fire. It intensifies to where I feel like I can't handle it anymore.

After you release God's healing power, trust in His love for you, and rest in His grace to sustain you. Even if His power feels overwhelming, don't ask Him to stop. Your heart *will* keep beating. He knows what you can handle, and He is not out to kill you.

Release the miracle healing power of God in you and upon you. Here's a prayer you can pray:

Heavenly Father, I enter Your throne room through the shed blood of Jesus Christ, Your Son. I ask for the miracle healing power of Jesus to permeate my whole life from the top of my head to the soles of my feet until I'm perfectly healed from cancer, arthritis, diabetes (whatever it is that you're dealing with). I command the spirit of infirmity in my fingers, colon, thyroid, eyes to leave my body in Jesus's name and come back no more. Amen.

Again, we do everything by faith, and I urge you to practice this. As you do it again and again, you will get used to and familiar with these principles. It's going to become part of your everyday life. Then you just do it anytime, anywhere, on the streets, at your place of work, without even thinking about it. Your boldness and confidence in God and in yourself are going to grow. That's why I encourage you to take action.

Pray for a creative miracle if you need one. If the doctors say you need a liver or kidney or pancreas transplant or a new eardrum, then ask God to give you a new one. The One who made you can replace those body parts with new ones.

Be specific in your asking. Access His storehouse by faith in the name of Jesus. Another simple prayer for a creative miracle could be:

Dear Heavenly Father, I enter the throne room through the shed blood of Jesus Christ. I'm asking You to take out this bad pancreas, heart, liver, and replace it with a brand-spanking new one in the name of Jesus. Amen.

PRAYER FOR DELIVERANCE

I command the spirit of fear, doubt, and unbelief to come out of my life through the blood of Jesus Christ. I now put on the Lord Jesus Christ and receive the fullness of His life, His faith, and power in me. In Jesus's mighty name, amen.

You see, it is simple and specific. Use this prayer as your starting point if needed as you believe God, and keep on taking action.

STEP 5: GIVE PRAISE AND THANKS TO GOD FOR HIS AUTHORITY.

Open your mouth and begin to praise and give thanks to God for answering your prayer. Thank Him for the authority He has given you to heal the sick and set people free, and that is including healing or setting yourself free. Continue thanking Him for His miracle healing power that is now at work in your life.

STEP 6: PUT YOUR FAITH INTO ACTION.

While you continue thanking God for healing and touching your life, get up and begin to put your faith into action. Do what you couldn't previously do whether or not the miracle is instant.

There comes a time when the enemy will attack your mind with questions such as, "Are you sure you're healed?" Your faith will be tested.

That is the point when you assure God that you believe His promise, that He does what He promised He would. You depend on that and stand on it, even if you haven't seen it yet. Remind the devil that the Bible doesn't say we'll see miracles and *then* we believe; the Bible says that these signs follow them who believe. I believe, and believing is our action. So act differently. Act what you believe. Act your miracle.

STEP 7: THANK GOD FOR FULFILLING HIS WORD

Continue thanking God for His integrity to fulfill His Word. Continue to confess your miracle and rest on God's promise.

If you need healing or deliverance, I encourage you to practice these methods on yourself. Release God's supernatural power on yourself, and you'll be amazed at what He does as you take action.

HOW MY HEALING
FROM DIABETES UNFOLDED

God said, "Andrew, have communion for seven days. Fast for seven days. Anoint yourself with oil for seven days, pray, and then get on a plant-based diet, and you will be healed."

There it was. God's healing strategy was quite different from what I had in mind. I didn't even know what a plant-based diet was.

On the way home, I picked up all of the prescriptions and supplies at the pharmacy. As soon as I got into my house, I took my first dosage of medication and insulin. Then I started to do what the Lord told me to do to get healed. I took communion with my family and anointed myself with anointing oil and prayed according to the above model.

You're going to use some or all of the methods I will be covering in the next chapter, Chapter 22 "Release Signs, Miracles, and Wonders Using Biblical Methods," to produce a miraculous witness in yourself as the Lord leads you. You're going to speak; you're going to exercise the authority and activate your faith with action in what God has promised. Lay hands and anoint yourself with oil. Have communion or seek God's miracle strategy.

For seven days, I partook in holy communion and anointed myself with oil. I cast out of my body the spirit of infirmity in my pancreas, in my cells and entire body that were manifesting into type 2 sugar diabetes. I also started the plant-based diet, which was similar to a vegan diet except without any kind of oil.

My blood sugar level went down. Within thirty days, my insulin and medication dosages were decreased by half. I continued thanking God every day for my healing, taking the insulin and medication to help with reducing insulin resistance.

After ninety days, I went back to my physician. He tested my hemoglobin A1C numbers, and it had dropped to 4.6 percent. The normal nondiabetic levels are between 4.0–5.6 percent. On that day, I was declared diabetes-free and healed.

My physician told me that in over twenty years of practicing medicine, he had never seen someone go from a blood sugar level of 560 to the normal levels of 110–120 within ninety days. There were high fives and congratulations as if someone had won a big prize. One of the nurses exclaimed, "This is historical!"

That was two years ago as of the writing of this book. Since then, I have been off insulin and all medication. I've continued on the plant-based diet and remain diabetes free.

In addition to my healing from diabetes, I lost the weight I previously couldn't lose. I remember asking God one time to help me lose the weight. "Lord, touch my metabolism to be normal," I said. I had tried exercise, eating healthy food, but I hadn't been able to quite get to my ideal weight. With God's strategy, I achieved both my healing and my ideal weight without much exercise.

The key was simple. I followed God's strategy above, and did what I could, and trusted Him to do what He alone could do. I learned that principle from the late Archbishop Benson Idahosa from Nigeria. Once preaching at a conference in Kampala, Uganda, he said, "Don't ask God to do what you can. That prayer will never be answered. The secret of doing the impossible is to do what you can, and let God do what you can't."

As a young minister, I took his words to heart and applied them. I found out he was right.

So, go for it. Follow these steps, and do what you can, and leave the rest up to God.

Now, join me in the next chapter as I reveal to you the biblical methods for releasing signs, miracles, and wonders through the anointing.

CHAPTER 22

Release Signs, Miracles, and Wonders Using Biblical Methods

"I'M HEALED! I'm healed!" she exclaimed excitedly.

I tested her, observing her walking back and forth and listening as she explained what had happened to her leg. Then out of the blue, she did a somersault and made a perfect landing on both feet.

This act caught me and everyone in the Encounter meeting by surprise.

Smiling, Rose said, "I couldn't help it."

Rose had told me that her left ankle had been snapped in half eighteen months ago. She had gone through treatment and physical therapy, but she couldn't put weight on her ankle due to the pain. She used a stick to help her walk, favoring her right leg.

Her mother-in law invited her to come with her to our monthly gathering. Rose didn't know what to expect, but my team had told her we would be praying for the sick.

So how did Rose receive her healing miracle from a broken ankle and from a skin disease she had since childhood? I'll tell you about that in a moment, but first let me show you the biblical methods of unleashing miracles, signs, and wonders through the anointing.

WE ARE IN THE SAME CLASS
AS JESUS AND THE APOSTLES

You can walk in the anointing and manifest the same miracles as Jesus and the apostles. I'm going to show you the biblical methods we can use today and see similar results as they did in the Bible. I discovered these methods over thirty years ago and have been using them ever since. They've produced miracles, signs, and wonders in my own life and in the lives of hundreds of thousands of people I have ministered to over the years. Whether it is one on one, in a church service, or in a mass gospel crusade, we have seen similar results when applying the same methods I'm teaching you here.

All truth is parallel. What worked for Jesus and the apostles will work for you and me today. If you get a hold of it, put it into your heart, and then let it come out through your mouth, hands, and feet.

Let me remind you what Jesus promised in the Great Commission in Matthew 28:18–19: "And Jesus came and spoke to them, saying, 'All authority has been given to Me in heaven and on earth. Go therefore and make disciples of all the nations, baptizing them in the name of the Father and of the Son and of the Holy Spirit, teaching them to observe all things that I have commanded you; and lo, I am with you always, *even* to the end of the age.' Amen."

You and I are in the same class of Jesus and the apostles. Why? Because Jesus gave us His power and His authority and power of attorney to use His name.

Jesus has breathed and continues to breath on us with His Holy Spirit. Let us see this in John 20:21–22 (TLB):

He spoke to them again and said, "As the Father has sent me, even so I am sending you." Then he breathed on them and told them, "Receive the Holy Spirit."

With the Holy Spirit now with us, upon us, and in us to anoint us, Jesus commissions us to work miracles in His name and power.

"Heal the sick, cleanse the lepers, raise the dead, cast out demons. Freely you have received, freely give" (Matthew 10:8).

You see, He has given you and me everything we would need to be successful in our lives and to fulfill the Great Commission in our world—where we live, work, and play. As the disciples obeyed and acted on the Commission, here is what happened:

And the apostles went out announcing the good news everywhere, as the Lord himself consistently worked with them, validating the message they preached with miracle-signs that accompanied them! (Mark 16:20 TPT).

Now, it wasn't the apostles working for the Lord but the Lord working with them and confirming their message with signs following them. They acted, and the Lord confirmed.

Even today, the Lord is working with you as you put into practice the following methods.

METHOD #1: SPEAK THE WORD IN FAITH AND WITH AUTHORITY.

What do I mean by the word? It's the word of healing, deliverance, the word of breakthrough, victory, and restoration. You have the promise of God's Word in your heart and mind, and now you're speaking that promise in faith and with the authority of the Lord's name.

When you pray for yourself or someone else, you use words. You cast out demons by the words you say. As we speak, the power of the Spirit is released to manifest the works of God.

> When evening had come, they brought to him many who are demon-possessed. And He cast out the spirits with a word, and healed all who were sick (Matthew 8:16).

How did He do it? Say it with me: "He spoke." Jesus cast the spirits out with a word, and that word is in your mouth—the word for healing, for deliverance, for salvation, and restoration.

Let's learn from our great Master, Jesus. He spoke the word to the demons. He said, "Come out!" (Matthew 9:32–33). To the blind, He said, "See!" (Luke 7: 21). To the deaf, He said, "Hear!" (Mark 7:32–33). To the paralyzed man at the pool, He said, "Rise up" (John 5:5). To the leprous man, He said, "Be clean" (Matthew 8:2–3).

HE PROMISED YOU GREATER WORKS.

> "In solemn truth I tell you, anyone believing in me shall do the same miracles I have done, and even greater ones, be-cause I am going to be with the Father. You can ask him for *anything*, using my name, and I will do it, for this will bring

praise to the Father because of what I, the Son, will do for you" (John 14:12–13 TLB).

That's right. He promises those who believe to do the same miracles, even greater ones. This was the basis of my book *Working the Works of God*.

"Then they said to him, what shall we do that we may work the works of God?" (John 6:28). You see, many leaders told me that wasn't true, that we aren't supposed to do greater works than Jesus.

"Do you mean that Jesus was lying?" I asked them. "Or do you mean He didn't intend to fulfill His promise because we won't believe?"

"No," they answered. "Jesus didn't mean it that way."

I decided I would believe what Jesus said in His Word and let Him tell me He didn't intend for me to do greater works. Dear friend, when you believe, you take Jesus by His word. You can live His lifestyle on His level.

I told you earlier that you're in His class, the class of power and of authority. You can step out of mediocrity, of obscurity, struggle, fear, and doubt and step into the class of power and authority where Jesus has opened the door for us.

Continuing on, John 6:29 tells us that "Jesus answered and said to them, 'This is the work of God, that you believe in Him whom He sent.'"

When we believe, we speak in faith and authority, thereby unleashing the floodgates of God's power and supernatural works on Earth as it is in heaven.

METHOD #2: EXERCISE YOUR DELEGATED AUTHORITY IN CHRIST.

Because you believed in Him, He said in His name, in the authority of His name, He has given you the power of attorney, the legal right that heaven and hell recognize when you use the name of Jesus. That's why in the *name of Jesus*, you can cast out demons.

> Then they were all amazed, so that they questioned among themselves, saying, "What is this? What new doctrine *is* this? For with authority He commands even the unclean spirits, and they obey Him" (Mark 1:27).

Wow. Why? Because he had authority from the Father. Now, you have authority from Jesus to use His name. Isn't that wonderful? You don't go out in your name. You go out in His authority.

> And they were astonished at His teaching, for His word was with authority (Luke 4:32).

Jesus's words had power, and so does yours. That's why it's crucial to know the anointing because the power of God is primarily released through words. The subject of God's precious anointing is so important that He led me to teach and record over thirty-three videos with forty-plus hours of training and activation to teach Christians how to receive the anointing, walk in it, and grow in it through the School of the Anointing online course.

When you cultivate a lifestyle of the anointing of the Spirit, then your words have power. Whether you just woke up from your sleep, whether you're on the street, your word carries the power, the dunamis, the dynamite of God, and you are releasing it because you know the authority you have.

Authority is in that name. Remember that the name is the active presence of an individual or entity. When you use the name of Jesus Christ, you bring His active presence into your situation and your midst.

Let's see what authority you have and what it does.

"Behold, I give you the authority to trample, to crush, to dismantle, to destroy serpents, scorpions, and demons, and over all the power of the enemy, and nothing shall by any means hurt you" (Luke 10:19, emphasis mine).

Look at yourself in the mirror. Miracle-working power that causes you to speak with authority is on your tongue, in your mouth, and in your words.

Now take a look at your hands. Those hands carry the authority of God. When you speak and lay hands on yourself and other people, the power of God, the authority of God is released through your mouth, through your members, through your hands. That's why you can confront the devil and prevail every time. Why?

Because you have the power. You have the authority, and you're using it.

Are you getting excited? I'm excited for you.

METHOD #3: EXERCISE YOUR FAITH.

Implement your faith in what you ask and in God's promises. Exercise your faith in the gospel, in what Christ has done in redemption for you at Calvary's cross.

Apply your faith in the finished work of Jesus, in His crucifixion, death, sufferings, burial, resurrection, ascension, and His present ministry in heaven at the right hand of God the Father. It's as simple as that!

> Then Jesus said to the centurion, "Go your way; and as you have believed, *so* let it be done for you." And his servant was healed that same hour (Matthew 8:13).

Matthew 8:13 was Jesus's response to what the centurion had said to Him in Matthew 8:8–9: "I'm a man in authority, so I know a thing or two about authority. You don't need to go to my house. Just speak." He believed the Word.

At the same time, He was exercising his faith in the words of Jesus. Then the miracle happened.

EXERCISE YOUR FAITH IN JESUS'S NAME.

Also exercise your faith in Jesus's name which carries His authority in you. We speak the name of Jesus.

We've already covered the power and the authority of the name, but it's worth repeating. When you exercise the authority in the name of Jesus, you're exercising and releasing the active presence of Jesus.

When you use His name in and with faith, miracles, signs, and wonders follow you.

> "And these signs will follow those who believe: In My name they will cast out demons; they will speak with new tongues; they will take up serpents; and if they drink anything deadly, it will by no means hurt them; they will lay hands on the sick, and they will recover" (Mark 16:17–18).

Why? Because the apostles believed in the gospel. They believed in what Christ has done, in what He said about them, in what He said He would do, and then they acted. They released the authority in the name. In the name of Jesus, they did it; in the name of Jesus, we can do it. We do everything by that name. How I love that name!

EXERCISE YOUR FAITH IN GOD'S PARTNERSHIP WITH YOU.

Exercise your faith in God's partnership with you. The Bible tells us that the Lord worked with them. Mark 16:20 says, ". . . the Lord working with *them* and confirming the word through the accompanying signs."

God is your partner, so you're sharing the divine resources that are at His disposal. As a result, you need to have faith in God's partnership with you and in His trust in you.

You need to believe that God has faith in you. He trusts you, and He's depending on you to do what He commissioned you to do. Also, we believe Him to be faithful to do what He said He will do to fulfill His promise for us.

When He says, "Go," your job is to go. He said you shall lay hands on the sick. Your job is to lay hands, not to produce the results. He's going to produce the results because He's working with you.

When you speak, He acts. When you stand still, He's going to stand still waiting for you to move. That's why he said, "Go. Act."

METHOD #4: RELEASE THE POWER IN YOUR HANDS.

The Bible says, "And these signs will follow those who believe: In My name they will cast out demons . . . they will lay hands on the sick, and they will recover" (Mark 16:17–18).

In the verse above, Jesus said that if we believe in His name and in His authority, we can simply lay our hands on the sick person in faith, and the power is released to heal them. We can also lay hands on ourselves and achieve the same results. The anointing in our lives is going to flow through our hands and touch whomever we're praying for.

Dear friend, this is your portion. This is not a monopoly of apostles and prophets, healing evangelists, or a chosen few in the body of Christ. It is for you as a believer.

Yes, some people have gifts of healings, working of miracles, and faith. Right now, though, what I want to awaken you to is the reality that you can walk in God's supernatural power through miracles, signs, and wonders today if you apply these principles I'm showing you.

METHOD #5: ANOINT WITH OIL.

It is scriptural to anoint with oil. "And they cast out many demons, and anointed with oil many who were sick, and healed *them*" (Mark 6:13).

In this book, I have shared with you several testimonies of miracle healings both for myself and for others to whom I have ministered, anointing them with oil and prayer. As you follow these methods, pay attention to the Holy Spirit. As you take action praying for yourself or others who need healing, breakthroughs, or victory, use oil and pray in faith with authority according to God's Word.

Is anyone among you sick? Let him call for the elders of the church, and let them pray over him, anointing him with oil in the name of the Lord. And the prayer of faith will save the sick, and the Lord will raise him up. And if he has committed sins, he will be forgiven (James 5:14–15).

Be free and allow yourself to enjoy the journey with God. Remember, you're partners with Him. Don't overthink it. Listen to the Holy Spirit. If He had told you, "Anoint with oil," and you don't hear anything else from the Lord at that moment, then follow everything He did tell you. Anoint with oil, and as you do it, the power is going to flow.

METHOD #6: DISCERN THE LORD'S BROKEN BODY THROUGH HOLY COMMUNION.

Two of my healing miracles came as a result of discerning the Lord's body. (Read about how to do this in Chapter 19 "Heal the Sick" and in Chapter 21 "Minister Healing and Deliverance to Yourself.")

Sadly, many of God's people have missed out on enjoying the healing and wholeness that Jesus has made available to us as we remember and recognize His broken body for our healing. We have already talked a lot about the blood. One of the primary purposes of the blood of Christ is for the forgiveness of our sins. (See Ephesians 1:7 and Hebrews 9:22.) But the Lord's body is for our healing, so we shouldn't confuse it with the blood. This misunderstanding has caused many in the Church not to receive what our Lord's body was broken for—divine healing and wholeness.

WHY ARE MANY CHRISTIANS STILL SICK?

By the Spirit of God, Apostle Paul told us why many Christians are sick, weak, and even die young—they have failed to properly discern the purposes of the Lord's body and what it suffered for our healing. When it comes to the blood, there are no arguments there. We all agree and believe that Jesus shed His blood for the washing away of our sins. But when it comes to the body, the misinterpretations of 1 Corinthians 11:28–30 has kept many away from correctly partaking. Let us read these commonly misunderstood verses that follow:

But let a man examine himself, and so let him eat of the bread and drink of the cup. For he who eats and drinks in an unworthy manner eats and drinks judgment to himself, not discerning the Lord's body. For this reason many *are* weak and sick among you, and many sleep.

Many have taken Paul's words "examine himself" and "unworthy manner" to mean sin. In a given church service, the minister would admonish the congregants to examine their hearts and see if there is sin that needs to be confessed before they approached the Lord's table; otherwise, they stand the risk of eating and drinking "judgment to himself." At that point, many people who are seekers or those still struggling with sin or habits dare not take communion.

I was in a church service once, and the brother next to me didn't take the communion elements as they were being passed around. When I inquired why, he said, "I'm dealing with some things in my life, and I don't want to bring God's judgement on me."

"Oh, I see," I replied.

At the end of the service, I briefly visited with him and talked about how the blood washes his sins away, and the body was for his healing.

He replied, "Well, I didn't know that. I just couldn't risk it."

I have since spoken to many people who have been taught that if you're struggling with sin, taking communion will cause judgement to come upon you. The part about examining your heart is about making sure you know why you partake at the Lord's table and the end result of forgiveness of sin and healing and wholeness. If you don't know what the blood and Christ's broken body are for, then you partake of the Lord's table in an unworthy manner. That's it.

Apparently, many in the Church repent of their sin before partaking of the elements but take it in an unworthy manner. That explains why even after taking communion, many are still weak, sick, and feeble.

HOW TO DISCERN THE LORD'S BODY

Christ's body was broken for our healing. When we accept, acknowledge, and receive by faith His finished work, we're discerning His body. Let us see a few verses to remind ourselves of what His broken body has done for us.

> Surely our sicknesses he hath borne, And our pains -- he hath carried them, And we -- we have esteemed him plagued, Smitten of God, and afflicted. And he is pierced for our transgressions, Bruised for our iniquities, The chastisement of our peace [is] on him, And by his bruise there is healing to us (Isaiah 53:4–5 YLT).

> . . . "He Himself took our infirmities And bore *our* sicknesses" (Matthew 8:17).

> who Himself bore our sins in His own body on the tree, that we, having died to sins, might live for righteousness—by whose stripes you were healed (1 Peter 2:24).

As we partake, the wine represents His blood, and the bread represents His body. We are accessing His divine life into ours.

As you hold that piece of bread in your hands, you recognize that His body was pierced, crushed, and bruised so that your body may be healed and made whole.

And as they were eating, Jesus took bread, blessed and broke *it,* and gave *it* to the disciples and said, "Take, eat; this is My body" (Matthew 26:26).

"Whoever eats My flesh and drinks My blood has eternal life, and I will raise him up at the last day. For My flesh is food indeed, and My blood is drink indeed. He who eats My flesh and drinks My blood abides in Me, and I in him. As the living Father sent Me, and I live because of the Father, so he who feeds on Me will live because of Me" (John 6:54–57).

When you partake of the bread, you're releasing your faith in what His body represents and carries for you. You are now joining your life with His and His life with yours according to the verse above.

PARTAKE IN HOLY COMMUNION AND CLAIM HEALING AND WHOLENESS.

Lord Jesus, I acknowledge and discern that Your body was broken for my healing. By faith, I now claim healing and wholeness in my body as I eat the bread. I receive Your divine life into my body until all sickness, infirmities, pain, and disease are perfectly healed. I thank you, Jesus, for divine wholeness that is now manifesting in my entire body. I love You and praise You for being my Healer now at work in my body. In Your mighty name, amen.

METHOD #7: SEEK GOD'S MIRACLE STRATEGY.

While I was experiencing liver failure, it was a huge surprise to me when I first heard the Spirit of the Lord speak to me, saying, "Ask

Me how I am healing you." I thought, *Why do you want me to ask? Just tell me.*

But then I asked Him as He instructed me to do so. The Spirit revealed His strategy for healing me and my family from the effects of the mold fungus. He pointed me to the blood and holy communion to discern Jesus's body. As a result, I experienced a creative miracle.

Then four years later when I got diagnosed with sugar diabetes, the Spirit said to me, "Ask me how I am healing you."

So I asked, and again I received specific instructions about what to do, how to do it, and how long to do it. (I shared the full story in Chapter 21 "Minister Healing and Deliverance to Yourself.") As I followed His strategy, my healing manifested three month later.

Why did God want me to ask Him how He was healing me? Because He wanted me to know that I am a son in His house, not a slave or a servant. I'm a member of His family. As my loving Father, He desires to show me what His will and strategy are for healing my family and me so that I could partner with Him in doing my part as He does His part. I've come to know that it's scriptural to inquire of or seek God's strategies for healing, victory, and blessings in any area of my life.

The Holy Spirit reminded me of Jesus and the secret to His success in life and ministry next to the anointing that was upon His life. The secret was that Jesus did on earth what He saw His Heavenly Father do.

> Jesus replied, "The Son can do nothing by himself. He does only what he sees the Father doing, and in the same way" (John 5:19 TLB).

The one key for Jesus to know His Father's secret was love.

"For the Father loves the Son, and tells him everything he is doing; and the Son will do far more awesome miracles than this man's healing" (John 5:20 TLB).

The same way God the Father revealed His secrets to Jesus because He loved Him is the same way Jesus reveals His secrets to you today because He loves you too.

In John 16:12–14 (TLB), Jesus promised, "But when he, the Spirit of truth, comes, he will guide you into all the truth. He will not speak on his own; he will speak only what he hears, and he will tell you what is yet to come. He will glorify me because it is from me that he will receive what he will make known to you."

Supernatural miracles and revelations of God's secrets to us are proof of God's love in Jesus Christ our Lord. Jesus, through the Holy Spirit, will reveal the secrets of God's love (Father, Son, and Holy Spirit) to you regarding any area of your life.

So before you start praying for a miracle, ask God and listen to what He says to you. He will reveal His strategy.

Most of the time, His way is different from what you might have had in mind. You're in a love relationship with God, and He cares about you, your family, your health, your finances, and your happiness more than you do.

DOUBLE-HEALING MIRACLES

I followed the same steps at the Encounter God's Power meetings with Rose, the lady who experienced healing in her left ankle at the beginning of this chapter. She had sat on the front row and listened intently as I preached a message entitled "The Lord Is Our Healer—Jehovah

Rapha," which was part of the teaching series on the Seven Miracles of Redemption. Rose believed in those miracles.

Afterward, I invited those who didn't know Jesus as their Lord and Savior to accept Him into their lives. That included those watching in our TV audience.

Then I invited the sick to put their hands on their area of pain, sickness, or disease. By faith, I raised my hand over the audience and prayed for their healing following the steps outlined in this chapter. I didn't lay hands on anyone. Next, I asked people to do actions they previously couldn't do.

Rose got up slowly from her seat and began to walk on both feet without help. The more she walked, the more she realized the pain wasn't there. She walked faster, stomped her feet, and felt no pain whatsoever.

When she came forward to testify on the microphone, she could hardly contain herself. She couldn't believe it. She kept stomping her feet, but that wasn't enough for her. She took a few steps backwards, and that's when she did that unexpected somersault, landing on the ankle that had been broken a few moments earlier.

"Oh," she said in utter amazement, "it's healed!" In fact, the power of God had perfectly healed her.

As she showed me what had happened with her ankle, she realized another miracle had also occurred. She noticed that with one touch, God had healed her of a skin disease that she had suffered from since she was young, and now she was in her late twenties with two children.

When she first arrived at the meeting, she didn't expect any of those miracles to happen. She left saved and rejoicing in the power of God.

The same principle applies to you if you need a miracle for yourself. Follow these simple but powerful biblical methods to unleash miracles. Or if you're ministering to others, the same steps will work as you apply action to your faith.

Like Rose, this healing and freedom by your faith is yours regardless of your spiritual gifting, maturity level, or calling. The anointing is in your life because the Miracle Worker and Healer lives in you.

Speak in faith. Use the authority you already have, and act in faith. The Spirit will move in your life and your world like never before.

Conclusion

CATCH AND RELEASE God's Supernatural was born out of passion and God's leading to help equip and teach laypeople and ministers about the kingdom power keys. It provides practical guidance to walk in miracles, healing, the gifts of the Spirit, and God's power in your life.

We have also created e-courses, programs, and a private online-training community to help take you deeper into these subjects. You can also connect with other like-hearted and passionate believers like yourself for encouragement and support.

My heart is to help you embrace the power that's already in you as you travel on this journey of activation of God's supernatural where you live, work, and play for His glory.

Now that you have finished reading *Catch and Release God's Supernatural*, it's time to get started. But where do you start?

The first thing you need to do is join *Catch and Release God's Supernatural's Monthly LIVE Mentoring with Dr. Andrew Nkoyoyo* so that I can help you go deeper beyond the book and create an action plan to practice each kingdom key daily for the next thirty days. The purpose of having action steps is to help you cultivate a lifestyle or form a habit of using these principles until they become part of your everyday walking-around life. I'll tell you more about this mentoring program later on in this book.

Contact Andrew for
CATCH AND RELEASE GOD'S SUPERNATURAL
Events, Conferences, and Workshops

DR. ANDREW speaks frequently on the topic of Catch and Release God's Supernatural. He can deliver a keynote, half-day, or full-day version of this content depending on your needs. If you are interested in finding out more, please visit his speaking page at:

kingdomimpactministry.org/speaking

For updates and resources, visit:
kingdomimpactministry.org/
Catchandreleasegodssupernaturalbook

Email: **Contact@kingdomimpactministry.org**

You can also connect with Andrew through his blog at:
Kingdomimpactministry.org/blog

Other ways to connect with Andrew are:
Twitter: **twitter.com/kingdomimpacttv**
Facebook: **facebook.com/andrewnkoyoyofan**
Facebook: **facebook.com/kingdomimpactministry**

Call: **1-855-41VOICE (418-6423)**

Join Catch and Release God's Supernatural!
Monthly LIVE Mentoring with
Dr. Andrew Nkoyoyo

See how you can experience and release miracles, healing, and the power of the Holy Spirit in your life and for other people much faster!

If you are serious about catching and releasing God's supernatural, maintaining and increasing in power, this is your next step.

What you get in this program:

- Every month, Andrew goes live for one to two hours to train you on a given topic.
- He will answer all your questions live.
- He will hold your hand, take you deeper, guide you step by step, and show you how to apply kingdom power keys, secrets, methods, and steps.
- Andrew will mentor you to catch and release miracles, healing, and power in your own life and for other people.
- You'll receive the recordings of the training in your member's area plus these bonuses: downloadable transcripts, audio MP3 files, and slides of every session for FREE!

You will join a private online community of like-minded and impassioned people like yourself for support and encouragement.

And you can cancel at any time...

Join now and reserve your seat today!

https://www.kingdomimpactministry.org/
Live-Mentoring

School of the Anointing
Online Course Program

CONTINUE LEARNING, and go deeper beyond this book. To continue mentoring you, Andrew recorded a comprehensive, accessible, and simple online training course entitled "School of the Anointing."

In this course, you will receive 40+ hours (33+ videos) of training and activation as he takes you deep into the topics discussed on the pages in this book and more. He not only shows you how to catch and release God's supernatural, but he also reveals how you can maintain and increase in God's supernatural power in your life.

Follow the web address below to watch a short video where Andrew personally talks to you and walks you through what to expect from this course. It comes with high-quality video training and a 24-7 member area that you can access anytime on any device.

Plus, you'll receive these free bonuses: audio MP3 files, training slides, transcriptions with action steps, and the activation of every lesson. Also, you'll be able to join a private online community and receive a certificate of completion.

Many serious disciples of Jesus have followed Andrew's advice to go deeper in power, miracles, and healing. Now you can too.

Ready to increase in God's supernatural power? Get started now at:

kingdomimpactministry.org/yes

Andrew's previous book:
Working the Works of God

Learn How to Walk in the Miracle Ministry of the Holy Spirit
(even if you're not in ministry)

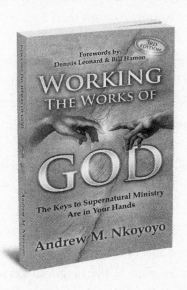

WHEN GOD'S power fell in the upper room in the Book of Acts, most of those in attendance didn't have an official ministry, yet they grabbed hold of it and walked in the ministry of miracles. God is calling out to you today, desiring that you too grab hold of that same power, no matter your role, title, job, and position, to supernaturally fulfill the calling on our lives.

For instance,

A woman blind from birth is instantly healed before an angry crowd who was ready to stone Andrew. Witnessing this miracle caused this same crowd to instead fall on their knees and repent.

As a woman riddled with AIDS lies on her deathbed, she becomes instantly healed, causing the doctors, nurses, and patients in the hospital to turn their lives over to God.

And these are only two testimonies told in *Working the Works of God*. In this groundbreaking book, Author Andrew Nkoyoyo answers the age-long question "What must we do that we might work the works of God?" With more than thirty years of fulfilling a miracle ministry around the world, he has experienced God's supernatural power both personally and in ministry. Consequently, within its pages, Andrew will mentor you on:

- How to receive power to move in the supernatural of God in a dimension like never before
- How to take hold of the kingdom keys to operate in God's supernatural, to work the miracles of God, including salvation, deliverance, healing, signs, and wonders
- How to walk in real prosperity and supernatural provision
- How to receive personal revival
- How to usher in revival for your family, friends, and nation, and so much more

God is calling you to the next level of His glory. Answer it, and get ready to be a changemaker, not only in your church but in the world!

Get your copy of *Working the Works of God* **at:**

https://www.kingdomimpactministry.org/ WorksofGodbook

"Dr. Nkoyoyo exposes the lies and accusations of the devil against God's saints. He presents the biblical truth that makes us free to be the man or woman God has called us to be. It is now time for all the saints and ministers to receive their inheritance... by working the works of God."

Dr. Bill Hamon
Bishop of Christian International Ministries Network (CIMN),
Author of *Day of the Saints* and eight other books.

Resources to Live a Holy and Supernaturally Empowered Life

ALL ACCESS PROGRAM

We have created an *all-access* program for you. Get unlimited access to everything, including all of our programs and library.

- You'll have 24-7 access to your member's area where you can log in and watch the content at your convenience anytime on any device.
- You'll have unlimited access to current and future content such as the "School of the Anointing" online course.
- You'll obtain access to special live mentoring to equip you to catch, release, and grow in power and in God's supernatural.
- You'll enjoy an inspiring and life-changing broadcast video message series and episodes to elevate your life, faith, and relationship with God.
- You'll receive training webinars, miracle testimonies, prophetic words, and so much more.

- Plus, you'll get bonus materials with the courses and training sessions for FREE!

Unlock everything when you subscribe today.

JOIN ALL ACCESS NOW

www.kingdomimpactministry.org/All-Access

Books and Resources
By Dr. Andrew Nkoyoyo

- Book: *Working the Works of God*
- Online Course: **School of the Anointing**
- Live Online Training: **Monthly Live Training with Dr. Andrew Nkoyoyo**
- Video Series: **Pursuing a Pure Heart Video Series: Results of a Surrendered Will to God**
- Video Series: **The Wonders of God's Glory**

Free Life-Changing Resources
Videos, Audio, Transcripts, and E-books

DID YOU KNOW that we have many free life-changing and inspiring messages that you can access online for free, such as videos, audio files, and e-books to elevate your life and walk with the Lord?

We believe they will help you fan the flame of God's gift and power in your everyday life!

Go to www.kingdomimpactministry.org/store

We Want to Hear from You!

I believe that through reading this book, you have been equipped to catch and release God's supernatural. We would love to hear how this book has impacted your life and/or your ministry.

Please share with us your biggest takeaways on our website at

www.kingdomimpactministry.org/contact

Become a Kingdom Impact Revival Partner with Me Today! Our "WHY" for the Glory of God

"Now more than ever before, people need Jesus. Together, we focus on bringing the world to Christ and preparing the Church, the bride of Christ, for His soon-to-be return to Earth."

—Dr. Andrew Nkoyoyo

And we need many partners like you to accomplish our WHY.

Jesus is coming back soon, and we must be ready! With your help, we will continue to be God's voice, "His trumpet on this earth," reaching people worldwide with the message of Jesus Christ.

What Is This Ministry Engaged In?

1. **BROADCASTING**—Through *Kingdom Come*, our weekly broadcast program, God's message is effectively touching millions of people around the world.

2. **KINGDOM IMPACT NETWORK**—People have access to our programs for free 24-7 from anywhere around the world on our website at www.kingdomimpactministry.org, Roku, Apple TV, Amazon Fire TV, Android TV, iTunes and Google Podcasts, apps for mobile devices such as tablets and smartphones.

3. **CRUSADES AND CONFERENCES**—Annually, Andrew ministers in several conferences and crusades around the world.

4. **RESOURCES**—With our books, teaching DVDs, CDs, MP3 files, video blogs (vlogs), training webinars, Bible studies, and devotional resources, we equip the saints for a holy and empowered life for the glory of God on the earth.

5. **MISSION OUTREACHES**—Our hearts are to meet the spiritual and physical needs of orphans and widows by providing food, clothing, and necessities through our partner churches and ministries in Africa, Asia, and Romania.

I personally invite you today to become a Kingdom Impact Revival partner with me in this ministry. Your monthly financial partnership makes it possible for us to continue bringing the world to Christ and to prepare the Church, the bride of Christ, for His soon-to-be return to Earth through our daily television broadcast *Kingdom Come*, strategic conferences, prophetic rallies, online media, teaching resources, mission outreaches, and with many more avenues. Without you, this would not be possible.

We are so excited for this urgent prophetic mandate for our generation that God has commissioned us to accomplish for His glory.

Won't you join us?

How do I become a Partner?

YOU CAN become a Kingdom Impact partner today by visiting our website www.kingdomimpactministry.org/partner and click on the "Donate" button. Enter your donation amount, check "monthly recurring donation," and enter your information.

As a partner, you unlock additional free resources, so thank you for deciding to partner with us, and together, we become the voice of Jesus Christ on the earth.

DONATE TODAY

www.kingdomimpactministry.org/Partner

Call us toll free at 1-855-41VOICE (418-6423)

About the Author

DR. ANDREW NKOYOYO is the founder and president of the Kingdom Impact Ministry. He is a revivalist, in-ternational speaker, host of the *Kingdom Come* television program, apostolic/prophetic minister, author, missionary from Uganda, East Africa to the United States of America. Additionally, Andrew is a member of Harvest International Ministry, an apostolic network. After many years of evangelistic, apostolic, and revival work in Africa, God called him into the mission field of America in mid-1999.

Andrew demonstrates a powerful anointing that has brought many people to salvation, healing, deliverance, and enabled them to engage in the power and gifts of the Holy Spirit. He trains, mentors, and equips the body of Christ to walk in the highest realms of God's supernatural power and glory.

He has impacted lives face to face in over twenty countries and reaches people daily in over 195 countries through his *Kingdom Come* broadcast program and streaming media. Andrew has shared miracle healing and revival stories on Sid Roth's television program

It's Supernatural. He has also shared the platform with speakers and Christian recording artists such as The Newsboys, For King and Country, Nick Vujicic, Jaci Velasquez, Sidewalk Prophets, Kutless, The Afters, Uncle Reese, and many more.

Andrew is the author of *Working the Works of God*, a book expounding on the keys to supernatural ministry. Together with his team, he carries the message of holiness, healing, and revival to America and the nations.

In his healing schools and in miracle crusade services, conferences, churches, festivals, media outreaches, and revival centers around the world, he ministers the gospel with manifestations of supernatural signs and wonders.

Andrew Nkoyoyo accepted Jesus as his Lord and Savior at age fourteen. His ministry began one year later when he prayed for a blind man, and God instantly healed him in front of the large crowd. At sixteen, Andrew held his first evangelistic gospel crusade, and by eighteen, he launched out in full-time ministry. Since then, God has been using Andrew in international healing and prophetic ministry. He has conducted gospel crusades and conferences in Africa, Europe, and North America.

Andrew was at the forefront of a prayer and outreach movement that ignited a nationwide transformational revival in his native country of Uganda, Africa. He is touching lives through his prophetic ministry and by demonstrating God's supernatural power. As a result, many are saved, healed, set free, and empowered to reach their God-ordained destiny.

In September of 2014, Jesus appeared to Andrew and commissioned him, saying, "Focus on being My voice. Bring people back to Me. Prepare them for My return, and call My church to awaken." For this reason, Andrew focuses on inspiring and impacting lives in the churches and communities toward a great spiritual revival that has the power to transform society by equipping people to catch and release God's supernatural love and power daily.

Andrew is married to Mona, and they have four beautiful children and make their home in Montrose, Colorado, in the United States of America.